Such a feast

spiritual nourishment and the churches

edited by

Judith Lampard

with

Chris Cook, Alan Horner, Paddy Lane
Christine Pocock, Diane Reynolds and Diana Simons

Churches Spirituality Group
Churches Together in England

2

Such a feast
Spiritual nourishment and the churches

ISBN 1 874295 17 4

Artwork by Chris Cook and Diane Reynolds

Printed and bound by Bath Press Ltd, Lower Bristol Road, Bath BA2 3BL

Contents

Introduction   5

Section 1: The Churches   9

The Baptist Union of Great Britain   11
The Cherubim and Seraphim Council of Churches   14
The Church of England   17
The Congregational Federation   21
The Council of African and Afro-Caribbean Churches   22
Oecumenical Patriarchate (Greek Orthodox)   26
Ichthus Christian Fellowship   31
The International Ministerial Council of Great Britain   34
The Lutheran Council of Great Britain   36
The Methodist Church   39
The Moravian Church   43
New Testament Assembly   46
The Council of Oriental Orthodox Churches   50
The Religious Society of Friends in Britain (Quakers)   54
The Roman Catholic Church   58
The Russian Orthodox Church   63
The Salvation Army   67
The United Reformed Church   70
The Countess of Huntingdon's Connexion   73
The Fellowship of Churches of Christ   75
The Free Church of England   78
The Old Baptist Union   80

Section 2: Individual Voices and Testimonies   83

Baptist   85
Black Pentecostal   87
Anglican   93
Members of The Countess of Huntingdon's Connexion   99
Methodist   102
Quaker   107
Roman Catholic   114
Russian Orthodox   123
URC   125

Section 3: Bodies in Association   129

Association of Interchurch Families (AIF)   131
Bible Society   134
CHAD (Church Action on Disability)   136
Christians Aware   138
The College of Preachers   141
The Focolare Movement   143
The Iona Community   146
L'Arche   149
Retreat Association   151
SCM (Student Christian Movement)   154
YMCA   156
Young Women's Christian Association (YWCA)   159

Endpiece   161

Information and Addresses   169

Index   173

Introduction

Such a feast reflects the wonderful variety of Christian spiritual nourishment in England at the beginning of the twenty-first century. This book, from the Churches Spirituality Group, is the latest stage in an ongoing process to help churches and individuals discern and share their 'spiritual treasures'.

Member churches of Churches Together in England were invited to identify the ways in which their members receive spiritual nourishment. We are pleased to include contributions from four members of the Free Churches Group, not themselves members of Churches Together in England, The Countess of Huntingdon's Connexion, The Fellowship of Churches of Christ, The Free Church of England, and The Old Baptist Union. The churches' responses to the question 'how are people nourished in the faith in your church?' are given in the first section of *Such a feast.* Their contributions are not formal 'official church statements' as such, but rather an attempt to identify and describe the distinctive emphases, traditions and spiritual resources of their particular church. It is not an easy task to provide a summary of the spiritual nourishment provided by a tradition, and we are grateful to all the writers. For at least one council of churches this involved translating its contribution into five different languages to get approval from all its members!

The churches have provided a remarkable tapestry of tradition, of word and symbol, of sacrament and service, of holiness and involvement, in the fullness of spiritual nourishment in the churches. The different traditions maintain their distinctive beliefs and practices, but there are also many common threads.

Individual Christians from a variety of churches provided the contributions which form the second section of *Such a feast.* Their voices and testimonies express a richness and complexity of spirituality with which many others can identify and, as some are quite personal, these are anonymous contributions. There was a determination to encompass, in this section, the wide range of Christian commitment, and we are pleased that this has been achieved. Christians of all ages, male and female, black, white and Asian, clergy and lay people, from city, village and town, and with a variety of Christian experiences, have written about their own spiritual nourishment.

It is clear from these personal accounts that some people discover their own tradition provides sufficient nourishment for their faith. Others find that their spiritual growth is enriched and deepened by the spirituality of other traditions. A third group find their spirituality is nurtured through their life experiences and personal relationships, more than their experiences of church life and worship. Some church traditions are not represented by individual contributions, although the invitation was extended to all, but this selection is nevertheless representative. We are grateful to all those individuals who have shared their own spiritual resources for their integrity, honesty and openness.

The final section of *Such a feast* has contributions from member Bodies in Association of Churches Together in England. These organisations, which bring together Christians of various traditions in a particular activity or area of special interest or expertise, were invited to share their distinctive spiritual insights. We are grateful to them for their challenging description of the spirituality which undergirds their work, and the spiritual nourishment provided.

The phrase *Such a feast* is taken from *The Call*, a poem by George Herbert, the seventeenth-century English poet. The image of a feast conjures up ideas of variety, plenty, richness, colour, nurture and celebration. Feasting is not a solitary activity, but enjoyed with others, and the feast is offered to all who read this book. *Such a feast* concludes with a brief section 'Endpiece', in which people who are familiar with the content of the book offer their reflections on it. We hope that readers will also want to reflect, alone or with others, on *Such a feast*, and on their own spiritual nourishment, as part of the ongoing exploration of sharing and exploring spiritual treasures.

The involvement of so many people in writing this book has provided the editorial group with some challenges, as well as delights. There has been an attempt to present the material in a clear and orderly way, although editorial policy has been influenced in part by a wish to be sensitive to the different traditions, for example in the initial capitalisation of letters. Most biblical quotations are from the New Revised Standard Version, although occasionally some writers have provided their own translations.

Members of the Churches Spirituality Group are grateful to all who have contributed to *Such a feast*. At a time when there is an acknowledged spiritual search among many in society for 'food for the soul', *Such a feast* indicates some sources of spiritual nourishment. It illustrates something of the richness, the plenty, the variety, the growth and nurture, that through God's grace, is available to all.

I would like to extend my personal thanks to past and present members of the Churches Spirituality Group, who have engaged with this project for over three years, and have shared their own spiritual journeys. The current members are Chris Cook, Brian Dwyer, William Green, Ruth Harvey, Jane Holloway, Alan Horner, Paddy Lane, Aziz Nour, Michael Playdon, Christine Pocock, John Rackley, Diane Reynolds, Christina Rees, Angela Robinson and Diana Simons. I am grateful to members of the editorial group for their enthusiasm and commitment; to Diane Reynolds and Chris Cook for their imagination and skill in providing the artwork; to Diana Simons for her painstaking work in compiling the index; and to Gill Stedman for her diligence and secretarial competence.

Judith Lampard
Maundy Thursday 2001

✠ The Churches

*describe how people are spiritually nourished
in their tradition*

The Baptist Union of Great Britain

Covenant

At the heart of our Baptist understanding of what it means to be the Church, is the theme of covenant. In the words of our covenant prayer we promise in the presence of God,

> *'To watch over each other*
> *and to walk together before you*
> *in ways known and to be made known'.*

Thus, our spiritual journey is one of accompaniment with God and one another, and faith and mission grow out of this covenant commitment, and find particular expression in a number of ways.

The Church Meeting

Baptist ecclesiology is rooted in the gathering together of the members of a local congregation. Membership and baptism are closely linked, as those who have been baptised into the faith also commit themselves to living out their discipleship among a particular group of people. The Church Meeting is the time when those in membership meet together as an expression of their covenant commitment to one another, and is the occasion when there is a shared process of discernment and decision-making. This is not a business meeting where only the loudest voices are heard or where a majority decision is sought, rather, it is a place where Christians listen to each other and to God, through prayer and reflection, in order to discern the mind of Christ.

Thus, the Church Meeting should be a place where believers are helped to grow in faith and where spiritual gifts are exercised. Each member has a responsibility for seeking the mind of Christ for kingdom purposes. Each member learns the discipline of listening to God and to others. Each member finds help and strength through this covenant relationship with the people of God.

It would be easy for such a congregational expression of church life to become insular. However, Baptist churches have always associated together, and this wider pattern of learning from one another is a source of spiritual breadth and diversity.

Prayer and Bible study

The discipline of personal prayer and Bible study is an important emphasis within Baptist life. The evangelical tradition of the 'quiet time' retains its place in popular spirituality, and priority is given to the necessity for all Christians to recognise their need for such spiritual nourishment.   The 'Word and Spirit' network exists particularly to support and encourage spirituality amongst ministers and leaders.

Over recent years, many Baptists have discovered and have come to appreciate the value of the retreat movement as a means of further enriching the personal encounter with God through prayer and scripture.

Core Values

Five Core Values for Gospel People was adopted by the Baptist Union in March 1998. It takes up the radical evangelical Baptist commitment to the biblical message and the centrality of Christ, and seeks to help Baptists understand their calling and identity for today.

We believe in following Jesus by living together as:
- a Prophetic community, confronting evil, injustice, hypocrisy, and challenging worldly concepts of power, wealth, status and security;
- an Inclusive community, transcending barriers of gender, language, race, class, age and culture, and identifying with those who are rejected, deprived and powerless;
- a Sacrificial community, accepting vulnerability and the necessity of sacrifice, and seeking to reflect the generous life-giving nature of God;
- a Missionary community, demonstrating in word and action

God's forgiving and healing love, and calling and enabling people to experience the love of God for themselves;

- a Worshipping community, engaging in worship and prayer which inspire and undergird all we are and do, and exploring and expressing what it means to live together as the people of God, obeying his word and following Christ in the whole of daily life.

It is our hope that these core values will guide and shape the way Baptists live their faith in the coming years as a people rooted in Christ and relevant to today's society.

Ecumenical Involvement

Our Covenant relationships are committed but not closed, and Baptists draw spiritual nourishment from many different sources. The freedom we have in liturgical practice enables churches and individuals to give expression to faith using the rich traditions of the Christian Church past and present.

Such gatherings as Spring Harvest, the Keswick Convention and Easter People attract large numbers of Baptists. The Iona Community has played a significant role in bringing together a concern for issues of social justice as part of worship, and the Northumbria Community has been formed with a specific Baptist identity. Our engagement with organisations like the Baptist Missionary Society, the Baptist World Alliance and Christian Aid brings us in touch with the world church. In all these ways, and many others, Baptist Christians are discovering and exploring new forms of spirituality.

The essence of covenant is relationship, and relationships are constantly forming and reforming. The image of journeying is thus fundamental to Baptist spirituality. At this present time the Baptist Union is seeking new ways of ordering its life and witness for a new century, and the hope is that these steps will give rise to fresh and life-giving expressions of what it means to live in unity with God and one another.

The Cherubim and Seraphim Council of Churches

Belief

This Church absolutely believes in Jesus Christ as the Son of God, in his birth, crucifixion, resurrection and ascension to heaven. We believe that God is One and has no equal. He is the creator of the Universe, Omnipotent, an Omniscient and Omnipresent Spirit, who is the beginning and the end of all things and beings. We believe in the supremacy and sovereignty of God the Father who by his word created heaven, earth, the sea, and all that dwells therein. We believe in Jesus Christ as the begotten Son of God who was with God in the beginning and without whom nothing was created (John 1).

We believe in the Holy Spirit and in Christ as Lord and Saviour who does his work through the Holy Spirit. This Church believes that the words of the Holy Bible were inspired and that men moved by the Holy Spirit spoke from God. It therefore accepts the Scriptures as the authoritative word of God. We believe in the truths set out in the three Creeds, the Nicene Creed, the Athanasian Creed and the Apostles Creed, for their foundation is in the Holy Scriptures.

History

Cherubim and Seraphim Church came into existence by divine revelations to St Moses Orimolade and to his assistant, Captain Ablodun Emmanuel, in Nigeria in 1925. Forty years later, in 1965, members of the Church who came as students to Britain established the Church in England, and it has grown progressively over the years. One of the distinctive features of the Church is the practical manifestation of the Holy Spirit, the Comforter, as truly revealed through the prophet Joel (Joel 2:28-32), and shown on the day of Pentecost (Acts 2).

Spiritual nourishment

Spiritual nourishment describes how the members (the worshippers) receive divine sustenance and enrichment from God by means of the Church's belief and doctrines, with teaching as its spiritual base. It is the result of spiritual exercise, and the result of light established in the soul.

The faith of church members is nurtured and enabled to grow by:

- The Bible - the readings, discussion, quizzes and seminars on the scriptures have immensely benefited our members.
- Spiritual revivals - centred on preaching, on holy songs and on receiving the Holy Spirit.
- Training of church workers has greatly enriched the Church. The membership is developed through the recently-established International School of Theology in London, and in other renowned Bible colleges. We provide Youth training and periodic camps for young people in the church (Proverbs 22: 6).
- Counselling - mature well-trained officials from various areas help members to resolve any difficulties and problems they may have.
- The Five-fold ministries of Apostleship, Prophecy, Evangelism, Pastorship and Teaching as defined by Paul in Ephesians 4:11 are fully used to nurture Christian maturity in the membership.
- Encouragement of marriage as a state instituted by God (Genesis 2:18; Matthew 19; Mark 10) has yielded impressive dividends.
- Baptism by immersion helps to nurture members' faith, convincing all that the Church is following Christ's teaching and example (Matthew 3:13-17; John 1:26-34).
- Holy Communion and the Lord's Supper are celebrated regularly, reviving and strengthening members' belief in the Lord, and a reminder that we are a part of the body of Christ. We extend such fellowship to the larger Christian community, recognising that the Church is part of the larger global Christian community (1 Corinthians 10; Matthew 26:26-29).

- Affectionate welfare - showing Christian love (1 Corinthians 13) through concern for the daily well-being of members has led to a dramatic growth in membership over the years.
- The maintenance of Christian discipline means adherence to God's laws and commandments (Exodus 20; 2 Timothy 2; Matthew 10; 1 Corinthians 5; and Galatians 6).
- Finally, prayers - which cement such nourishment into the hearts and lives of the membership.

Empowered by the Holy Spirit

Members recognise that God established the Cherubim and Seraphim Church in Africa, using miracles to show the practical manifestation of the Holy Ghost, thereby converting unbelievers from their heathen gods. Pentecostal flames helped to destroy the heathen customs and fetish practices. The Cherubim and Seraphim Church proclaims that Jesus is 'the Way, the Truth and the Life' (John 14:6), and 'God is Spirit, and those who worship him must worship him in Spirit and in Truth' (John 4:24). This Church uses the word of God to nurture the faith and growth of membership (1 Timothy 4:6; James 5; Colossians 2:19). Above all, it is the Holy Spirit that enables such nourishment and enrichment (John 6:63). Through divine revelations, the Lord promised to use this Church to spread his Holy Spirit into every nation of the world.

The Church of England

Like the Anglican Communion, to which it belongs, the Church of England embraces a wide range of resources and styles that sustain its people spiritually. Its services include elaborate ceremonial and liturgical simplicity, formality and occasions of spontaneity. The resources for personal spirituality and prayer that are available to Anglicans are truly ecumenical.

Resources

The Bible is held to contain all things necessary to salvation. It is extensively read in worship and provides the Psalms and many of the Canticles that, together with Scripture readings (Lessons) and prayers structure Morning and Evening Prayer. Personal Bible reading also sustains Anglicans in their Christian life.

The Book of Common Prayer (1662) comprised the whole of Anglican worship until fairly recently and has left a permanent stamp on it. The author of the Prayer Book tradition, Archbishop Thomas Cranmer, simplified the medieval Hours, reformed the theology, but retained the early prayers and canticles from Eastern and Western traditions. *The Book of Common Prayer* is still much used, especially for Evensong, and its authority, along with that of the Thirty-nine Articles and of the Ordinal, continues as a doctrinal standard and liturgical benchmark.

The Alternative Service Book (1980) codified experimental modern language services and became the staple diet of most parishes. However, it has not worn well and has recently been replaced by the new services of *Common Worship (2000)*. An unfamiliar feature was the selection of Eucharistic Prayers, and this aspect is reproduced in *Common Worship*. The latter sets out to offer a more robust, three dimensional liturgical language, with more scope for seasonal and occasional alternatives in non-core aspects of the liturgy, than *The Alternative Service Book*. Other supplementary liturgical material authorised by the General Synod is available.

Celebrating Common Prayer is widely used for the daily offices and informal use is made of various kinds of supplementary material.

A rich tradition of hymnody includes hymns of the Early Church in translation, many hymns of Charles Wesley, Victorian old favourites and twentieth-century hymns and songs. The greater informality and spontaneity of some Anglican worship reflects the influence of the charismatic movement. Cathedrals, Westminster Abbey and St George's Chapel Windsor, major parish churches, and college chapels maintain a distinctive choral tradition of musical excellence.

The Christian Year

With its pattern of festivals and saints' days and seasons of preparation and penitence (Advent and Lent), the liturgical year provides a central resource for the Church of England. Important pastoral opportunities are created by such national and family occasions as Remembrance Sunday, Mothering Sunday, Harvest Festival, 'Midnight Mass' and services of Lessons and Carols at Christmas.

Some distinctive characteristics of Anglican worship and spirituality

There is a complementarity of Word and Sacrament. In parish churches, the altar is either at the East end or, more likely today, in the nave. It is framed by the pulpit and the lectern and balanced by the font which is usually near the entrance or at the West end. The Eucharist has become the central service in most parishes, but Family Services and special services, such as Harvest Festival, are seen as providing access for non-communicants. Though the emphasis varies from parish to parish, Anglican spirituality is marked by an integration of Word and Sacrament.

There is an inclusivity of approach. The experience of fellowship that undergirds Anglican spirituality is often focused on the parish church and churchyard, thus setting it at the heart of the local community. The lack of any formal concept of membership and the deep involvement in the life and concerns of the community give, at best, a sense of hospitality and openness to Anglican spirituality. Anglican inclusivity is pastoral and orientated to mission. While the importance of commitment and discipleship is fully recognised, the Church of England works with a far more diffused sense of belonging than is found in most other churches.

Anglican worship affirms the faith of the Church in various forms that have been handed down from the early Church. The Apostles' Creed is said at Morning and Evening Prayer and the Nicene-Constantinopolitan Creed is said or sung at the Eucharist. Shorter declarations of faith are made at baptism and may be used at other services. In much Anglican worship there is a strong sense of the continuity of tradition. One example of this is the continuing contribution of religious communities to Anglican spiritual life.

Rites of passage

The Occasional Offices (baptism - both infant and adult - confirmation, marriage, and funeral rites) play a large part in Anglican spirituality and help to structure it by relating Christian beliefs to stages on the journey of life. They tie in with the Christian Year, as new birth in baptism is grounded in the Incarnation, celebrated at Christmas, and the comfort of Christian hope for the dying and bereaved is grounded in Christ's death and resurrection, proclaimed in Holy Week and Easter. These Occasional Offices provide parish clergy with many welcome pastoral contacts and opportunities for Christian teaching.

Lay participation

Although there are strict rules that confine certain aspects of ministry to clergy, and public worship is under the oversight of the diocesan bishop, Anglican spirituality is, on the whole, not clerical. In the sixteenth century the principle that the laity should participate intelligently in the church's worship led to the translation of the Scriptures and the liturgy into the vernacular. Lay people play a major part in the conduct of worship and there are officially recognised lay ministries (especially that of Reader, Church Army Officer and Lay Parish Assistant) which play a vital role in the flourishing of collaboratative ministry. Lay personal spirituality is nourished by private Bible-reading and prayer.

Consecration of God's gifts

The use of fine buildings, music, flowers, liturgical colours, vestments, crosses, crucifixes, pictures and statues, occasionally incense, and physical movement in worship is important for many Anglicans. It represents the consecration of God's good gifts in creation to the worship of God. Worship, though it is nothing unless it comes from the heart, needs outward, visible expression: it is sacramental. The corollary is that all our senses can be caught up in adoration. Anglican spirituality, whether ornate or austere, is meant to involve the whole person.

The Congregational Federation

Training

The Congregational Federation has an integrated training course, which provides training for people at all levels. In the training for ministers and pastors (lay leaders), attention to spiritual development is encouraged. The candidates are invited to keep a journal which they discuss with their tutor at each training weekend. Some modules and some weekends focus on spirituality.

Spiritual Nourishment

In this way ministers are also trained to help in the spiritual nourishment of the congregations to which they may be called in ministry. But members of congregations may also take up the training course for one to four years - moving on as they wish - and each level includes attention to spiritual nourishment, including worshipping together at course weekends, and introduction to useful resources.

Resources

As well as making ecumenical resources available, such as the United Reformed Church's *Prayer Handbook* and ecumenical Lent material, the Congregational Federation produces occasional resources. *Transformations* and *Head, Heart, Hands* were both group study courses and included material for prayer and reflection. *Peculiar Honours,* a hymn resource, includes notes linking the hymns with the history of their writers and the context in which they were written. *Gatherings* is a regular resource which includes material for congregational and private use.

The Council of African and Afro-Caribbean Churches (CAACC)

Belief

In the African Indigenous Churches spirituality is understood to refer to the interaction between humans and God in their striving to have the character of Jesus. The goal is to 'come to the unity of the faith and of the knowledge of the Son of God, to maturity, to the measure of the full stature of Christ' (Ephesians 4:13). Spiritual nurture refers to all the activities of the churches with this aim. It is understood to be characterised by the tension between what is (the human predicament of sin and disobedience, alienation and misery) and the higher state (having the character of Christ) towards which one strives. However, no antithesis between the higher and lower selves is implied, but rather a continuity or progression from what is to what could be.

Side by side with the internal quality of the individual (what St Paul describes as having the fruits of the Spirit), spiritual nurture is also understood in terms of the nurturing of the spiritual gifts in a person – such as healing, prophesying, interpreting dreams and discerning spirits. Therefore it is not only spiritual awareness, or even inner peace that they strive for, but a practical engagement in the activities of the Holy Spirit, by whose agency they believe they can achieve life's fullness.

There are several resources for spiritual nurture in the Church, to enable the members' personal spiritual experiences. Such spiritual experience is understood as a reality that can only be interpreted in terms of a mediated presence of the Divine, or the taking over of the voluntary capacities of the individual as he or she is filled by the Spirit of God. In this way it is understood that the Transcending God impresses himself upon humans, and the human response is a voluntary abandonment of the self, the will and action to the movement of the Spirit of God as his presence is manifested.

Worship

Worship in the African Indigenous Churches is essentially an affirmation of faith and the rendering of praise and thanks. The exuberant nature of worship in the churches comes from a feeling of awe, and is an expression of self-abandonment. It is expected that from the harmonious singing and dancing and the collective prayers, worshippers are led to a state of much deeper harmonious functioning, where the church functions as one body.

As worshippers consciously submit themselves to worship, they are impressed by the joy brought by God's overwhelming presence through the Spirit, and feel completely invigorated, reassured, and quickened by the Spirit. God is experienced in worship and there is a belief that one does come to know God through praising him, praise preceding knowing.

Services for Holy Spirit revival are important for spiritual nourishment. In these special services the members are brought to the position where they experience truths about God, and are put in touch with the reality of the Spirit of God. Those truths about God do not derive from empirical historicity, or necessarily from Scripture, but from God's active and ongoing dealings with his children, dealings which confirm to them that God is love, eternally and actively loving, and that God does still reveal himself and his will to his children. Spiritual nurture is therefore an exercise in discovering and participating in the love of God.

Fasting and prayer are widely practised in these churches. In some of them there are regular days in the week where all members are expected to observe a fast. There are congregational fasts and individual fasts, sometimes accompanied with confinement for intensive prayers. Fasting is taught as a discipline that focuses attention on God, and a necessary self-deprivation that brings urgency to prayer.

Individual Lifestyle Guidance

Most daily experiences of life are seen to have a religious dimension -
in this case, a God-dimension. Nothing is believed to take place
outside of God's knowledge or control, and study sessions,
exhortations, and testimonies by ordinary members provide means for
re-orienting the members in their behaviour and character. Closely
related to this is a strong belief in the existence of evil spirits. There is
awareness in the churches of the pervasiveness of evil forces or
spirits, who fight against the children of God, seeking to destroy
them. There is a strong belief in the active working of the Holy
Spirit, whom Christians can beseech to perform services for them,
and free them from Satanic forces. To them this is not just a belief
but an actuality attested to by daily experience. What the churches
teach is that staying with God is the best protection from evil forces.
Therefore leading a good life is enjoined not only because of the
desire to go to heaven, but because of the belief that leading a good
life frees one from the influence of evil forces.

Spiritual Counselling and Consultation are among the tasks assigned
to pastors or prophets/prophetesses in the African Indigenous
Churches. These are essentially one-to-one sessions involving the
minister and a church member, in which the minister attempts to help
the member understand the meaning or implication of, or message
contained in, a spiritual experience that the member may have had. It
is expected that the minister will himself or herself be a person with
deep and sound spiritual insight. The session employs counselling
skills and the spiritual gift of discernment. It places no weight on
psychological interpretations, but relies heavily on intuitive
perception of spiritual guidance. Therefore it does not pay much
attention to internal psychic processes but focuses on divine
communication and the recipient's required action or response.

Bible study in the churches is more a case of sharing than teaching.
Participants share their faith and what God has revealed to them.
Scripture is therefore seen as a guide, helping the participants to
understand real and everyday phenomena. The space in worship for

testimonies and impromptu exhortations is to enable this sharing to take place. But it is even more the case in Bible study sessions. The churches believe in the inspiration of the Scripture, seeing in the pages God's own free decision to communicate his word. There is usually no questioning of the validity or truth of any part of Scripture, and there is an absence of unhelpful debate – unhelpful in the sense that it does not edify, or that it is based on human thinking instead of spiritual revelation.

The work of the Holy Spirit

Spiritual nurture is to create a hunger, as well as to satisfy a hunger, for the Holy Spirit. The rationale for this is based on 'Ask, and it will be, given you; search, and you will find, knock, and it will be opened for you' (Matthew 7:7). What members ask for is the agency of the Holy Spirit in managing the affairs of life. The African Indigenous Churches are therefore called 'Spiritual churches' or 'praying churches' in West Africa because of their inclination for pneumatological interpretation of Scripture, as well as the claim to reliance on the Holy Spirit in all matters relating to church and public life.

In the African Indigenous Churches, spiritual nurture is achieved through participation by the individual in the corporate activity. The minister's role is best understood as creating the material condition that allows this growth to take place.

Oecumenical Patriarchate (Greek Orthodox)

The Archdiocese of Thyateira and Great Britain (from which this contribution derives), as a Diocese under the Prime See of Orthodoxy, the Oecumenical Patriarchate of Constantinople (to which it looks as its Mother), is part of the worldwide Orthodox Church that, in addition to the Church of Constantinople, includes the historic Patriarchates of Alexandria, Antioch and Jerusalem, as well as the Russian, Serbian, Romanian, Bulgarian and Greek Orthodox Churches, and the Orthodox Churches of Cyprus, Georgia, Poland, Albania, and the Czech lands and Slovakia. Many Christians in those parts of the world where there are no National Churches look to the Mother Church of Constantinople for spiritual sustenance and support (as do the Churches of Finland and in Estonia); and in these Islands the Archdiocese of Thyateira and Great Britain embraces communities whose ethnic origins are not only from the four nations of England, Scotland, Ireland and Wales, but also from Greece, Cyprus, Belarusia, Latvia, Romania, Turkey, Egypt, and elsewhere.

Orthodox Christians believe that they belong to the One True Church of Christ and that they bear witness to him through Orthodoxy (that is to say 'right belief' and 'right worship'). They therefore live in union with the Mystery 'that has been hidden throughout the ages and generations' (Colossians 1:26), but which has now been 'revealed to (Christ's) holy apostles and prophets by the Spirit' (Ephesians 3:5).

The heart of Orthodoxy

The spring that nourishes and sustains Orthodoxy is Holy Scripture and Sacred Tradition - the former being seen as 'the very substance of the dogmas and liturgies of the Orthodox Church and (which), through them, impregnates the piety of Orthodox souls' (Lev Gillet) and the latter as 'the Life of the Holy Spirit in the Church' (Vladimir Lossky), 'the constant abiding of the Spirit and not only the memory of words' (Georges Florovsky). This source is an inseparable unity and not two contrasting and conflicting elements.

From Holy Scripture, we find encouragement not only for our daily life but also for our worship - as we read passages that relate to the meaning and significance of the particular day or are inspired to create the hymns and praises that are chanted day by day. From Sacred Tradition, we have received Holy Scripture itself together with its interpretation through the God-inspired Fathers of the Church and a deeper understanding of the teachings of the Faith. The Orthodox Church is thus seen as 'the Holy Catholic and Apostolic Church founded upon the Apostles and preserved by the divine and inspired Fathers in the oecumenical Councils, having as its head Christ the Great Shepherd, who purchased it with his blood; and that (according to the inspired and heaven-bound Apostle) it is the pillar and ground of the truth and the Body of Christ. This Holy Church is indeed one in identity of faith and similarity of manners and customs, in unison with the decisions of the seven oecumenical Councils, and it must be one and not many, differing from each other in dogmas and fundamental institutions of ecclesiastical government' (to quote the words of Patriarch Joachim III and the Holy Synod of the Patriarchate of Constantinople in 1902).

Prayer

Prayer and fasting are central to the life of a true Christian. As Orthodox Christians we would use not only those forms of prayer that are to be found in Holy Scripture but also those prayers that have been handed down from generation to generation or composed in more recent times. The hymns chanted during our worship (and also used in private prayer) may, in some cases, be of ancient origin but in others may well be far more recent or even written during the last few years. Orthodox Christians worship both as a Family in church and with the family at home with their prayerful worship being understood as a unity (that is to say, with no distinction between public prayer in church and private prayer at home, just as there is no distinction between the prayer of the home and the prayer of monastics). Fasting is seen as the training and disciplining of the body, Man being understood as a unity of soul and body. Prayer, fasting and 'the amputation of our desires through humility of soul, inactivate the spirit of self-indulgence (which we overcome) through tears of repentance and, shackling it with self-control, render it immobile and ineffective' (Nikitas Stithatos).

Most Orthodox Christians find that they are able to focus their prayers better when they are in the presence of icons - whether in the sacred surroundings of a church with its decoration reminding the believer that it is 'heaven on earth,' or in the special place of prayer set aside in his or her own home. Iconography has its own 'mystical language' which speaks directly to the heart, which is why the presence of an icon is helpful. However, the icon also has its dogmatic character in that it depicts visually the faith and teaching of the Church, emphasising the Incarnation of Christ. To quote St. John of Damascus, 'Now that God has appeared in the flesh and lived among men, I make an image of the God Who can be seen'. However, we carefully distinguish between 'the relative honour or veneration shown to material symbols, and the worship due to God alone' (St John of Damascus).

But the true 'Prayer of the Heart' is the Jesus Prayer: *Lord Jesus Christ, Son of God, have mercy on me* (to which some people add *a sinner).* It has been described as 'a prayer of marvellous versatility (in that it is both) a prayer for beginners, but equally a prayer that leads to the deepest mysteries of the contemplative life (and which) can be used by anyone, at any time, in any place: standing in queues, walking, travelling on buses or trains; when at work; when unable to sleep at night; at times of special anxiety when it is impossible to concentrate upon other kinds of prayer' (Timothy Ware).

The life of an Orthodox Christian is surrounded and protected by prayer since we ask the blessing of the Triune God on all that we do. It is to God that we turn on waking: *On rising from sleep, we fall down before you, O Good One, ...;* and it is to him again that we turn when going to sleep: *Into Your hands, Lord, I entrust my soul and body.* Our whole day is therefore lived in his presence.

The Mysteries

In addition to prayer, our spiritual life is strengthened and deepened through regular and sincere participation in the Mysteries (or Sacraments) of the Church - principally through reconciliation with the Triune God by way of Repentance ('Metanoia') and the worthy reception of the Body and Blood of Christ in the Eucharist ('Eucharistia'). When we have bodily or spiritual ailments, we ask to be anointed with Holy Oil ('Euchelaion'). Among the other Mysteries are: Entry into the Christian Family through Illumination - that is Baptism and the imposition of Chrism (Chrismation) that is performed immediately afterwards; the creation of a new Christian family in Marriage; and the setting apart of Sacred Ministers through ordination to the Diaconate, Priesthood and Episcopate. In addition, our spiritual life is enriched through the study and discussion of the writings of the Fathers of the Church and of other inspired Teachers (including those living in the century that has just passed). In addition, we read the lives of the saints - holy men and women, friends of God - and celebrate their feasts, honouring them by trying to put their example into practice in our own lives. Many Orthodox Christians would look to a specific 'Spiritual Father' or 'Elder' (often, but not always, a monastic) for advice in their spiritual endeavours, attaching considerable significance to his guidance.

Our Orthodox spirituality has been described as having the principal characteristics of 'asceticism, humility, tender-hearted brotherly charity, an eschatological dream of the City of God shining with righteousness and spiritual beauty' (Prof. A.V. Kartashev). This 'vision' is the fruit of the spiritual nourishment that we receive from the Church, albeit with its characteristic of joy in the face of pain, an heroic and militant spirit, and 'the fervent expectation of the Parousia'. However, having said this, it has to be emphasised that it is impossible to describe the two-thousand-year uninterrupted experience of Orthodox spiritual life and nourishment in a few lines. What can be said is that the Passion and Resurrection of Christ have given a new dimension and expectation to the world and to our everyday life.

Ecumenical participation

Christians have also received the command to proclaim their faith, thus spiritually nourishing the nations. Indeed, it is this instruction from the lips of the Risen Lord (contained in Matthew 28:16-20) that is quoted in the Gospel passage read during the Baptismal service. Despite the uniqueness of our Faith, Orthodox Christians participate in what has become known as the 'Ecumenical Movement' believing 'it is right to help (those who are heterodox) as much as possible to fight the good fight, in order that, inclining neither to right nor left, they may seek after the way which leads directly to the Orthodox Church' (Patriarch Joachim III, as above), thereby helping others to enrich their own spiritual lives and come to a full knowledge of Him Who is the Way, the Truth and the Life (John 14:6) and 'Who has raised up an ensign (see Isaiah 5:26) to the ages through His Resurrection ... in the one body of His Church' (St. Ignatius, *Epistle to the Smymaeans 1*).

Further Reading:

Timothy Ware (now Bishop Kallistos of Diokleia), *The Orthodox Church*, Penguin Books, Harmondsworth, 1963.

Ephrem Lash (comp. & trans.), *An Orthodox Prayer Book*, Oxford, 1999.

Ichthus Christian Fellowship

Ichthus Christian Fellowship ('Ichthus') is an evangelical, charismatic church which has local churches/congregations in London, throughout the UK and a few overseas. Ichthus subscribes to the Basis of Faith of the Evangelical Alliance.

Purpose

In Ichthus, we seek by many means to nurture and deepen **both** the corporate expression of our love for God and one another and of our witness to the world (Mark 12:29-31) **and** every individual's relationship with God, Father, Son and Holy Spirit. Central to all that we do is our worship of God, study and proclamation of the Word of God (the Bible), prayer, evangelism through both word and action, and fellowship. In the context of all these, we want to be like Jesus, to see the development of the fruits of the Holy Spirit (Galatians 5:22-23) and the exercise of the gifts of the Holy Spirit (Romans 12:3-8; 1 Corinthians 12:7-11). We want to express the words, works and wonders of Jesus to the world around us. We have tried to structure Ichthus to maximise our effectiveness in doing all this.

Structure

We meet in local churches/congregations for worship, Bible teaching and prayer, and these groups are sufficiently big to impact local neighbourhoods and communities with the love of Christ. Local congregations provide the context for the dedication of young children, baptism of adults who give their lives to Christ, the taking of communion, children's work and youth activities, weddings and funerals. The congregations are divided into homegroups/cells which are small units providing more intimate fellowship, prayer and support. In London, we hold monthly celebrations where all our London congregations meet to worship and are taught from the Bible. This provides a large meeting to strengthen people's faith and to produce an awareness that we form part of the Church of Christ worldwide. Once a year, we hold a camp for all our churches, Revival

Camp, providing inspirational worship, bible teaching, seminars, workshops and leisure activities.

Our worship makes use of music, dance, drama and poetry, all designed to help people focus on God and to develop a lifestyle of worship and service in our everyday lives. Songs are drawn from the wealth of hymns written over the centuries and from contemporary writing.

We have people working overseas and all members are encouraged to be involved in some way (by praying, giving and/or going) in God's work throughout the world.

Discipleship

We want to meet the spiritual needs of people from the non-Christian enquirer to the committed disciple of Jesus. We make use of the Alpha courses. We have produced a twelve-week discipleship course, 'Startrite' for new Christians. We encourage people to be in a one-to-one discipling and mentoring relationship, giving and receiving biblical teaching. We promote personal prayer and study of the Bible as essential to personal spiritual growth, and we encourage people to practise the traditional spiritual disciplines, including fasting. Giving financially on a regular basis to support the work of the local church and the Church worldwide is seen as an important part of worship and service.

We provide varied opportunities to people to share the Gospel with non-Christians and this includes not only speaking to others but also practical acts of service in the name of Christ. In addition to such social action, we encourage people to think about how their faith affects social and political issues, local, national and international, and, where appropriate, to take action. We believe that there should be no divide between the sacred and secular, working to ensure that our faith and worship infuse every aspect of our lives.

Pastoral Care and Training

Acknowledging that all of us need help to develop and live in the world in God's way, we provide pastoral care through cells and congregations and make other particular provision in areas of need that we find people have. This takes the form of counselling, prayer for healing (physical, emotional and spiritual), personal wholeness courses, renewal for Mums, divorce recovery groups, marriage preparation and marriage development, a pregnancy prayer chain, and support for those suffering from mental health problems.

We provide leadership training for congregation leaders and cell leaders. We are running a monthly Bible school for Ichthus members (full day, Saturday). We have a month-long training course each summer, 'July Project', and a year-long training course 'Network'. Usually, twice a year, we provide a mini-course for leaders, 'Restoring spiritual vision'. We produce literature, audio and video tapes of teaching for borrowing or purchase. We produce a quarterly magazine containing inspirational articles and personal stories.

All that we do as a church is intended to deepen our relationship with God and our relationships with each other, and to demonstrate to the non-Christians around us that God loves them.

International Ministerial Council of Great Britain (IMCGB)

Nurture

In the International Ministerial Council of Great Britain (IMCGB), each Church body is autonomous and therefore practices vary.

Practices are, however, based on Bible study, and individual and group prayers are seen to be a key factor in spiritual nourishment.

Occasions when nurturing takes place are week-night and Sunday Bible study and prayer meetings, praise and worship sessions in the Church services, preparation for baptism, counselling, children's Sunday School, choir practices, training classes for leaders, prayer and laying-on of hands 'ministering' sessions, sometimes with prophesying, in Church services or home visits, visits to the sick, prison visits, church projects, daily prayers in the church office, sermons and all elements of the church services.

We encourage individuals to seek the gifts of the Spirit and to exercise them.

The IMCGB holds ministers' conferences with prayer, Bible study and discussion, teaching and sharing of experiences to assist leaders. Bishops are also available to counsel ministers who seek any kind of help.

We believe this nurturing is for a purpose, to equip us to spread the Gospel.

Life in the Spirit

In all these ways we teach people to recognise the work of the Holy Spirit in their lives and to give thanks for the resultant blessings. Living a Spirit-filled life as outlined below, and recognising the presence, leading and empowerment of God, with resulting joy and peace and fellowship in worship is what we understand by 'spirituality' – a foretaste of the bliss of Heaven.

Some basic concepts from God's Word

Life in the Spirit starts with repentance and new life in Christ (John 3:5-8; Acts 2:38). It is about being made holy (Hebrews 10:10; Romans 12:1-2). It belongs to and is the well-spring of the life of faith described by Jesus (Luke 9:23; John 3:8).

Life in the Spirit is the means of our relationship with Christ, by which we bear fruit (John 15:5). It produces fruits of character which enable community interdependance (Galatians 5:22) and is fed by fellowship, Bible study and prayer (Romans 8:26; 2 Timothy 3:14-17).

Life in the Spirit is displayed in gifts of the Spirit which enable the Church to do the work begun by Jesus, that is, to carry out the Great Commission (1 Corinthians 12:4-11; Ephesians 4:11-13).

'Like good stewards of the manifold grace of God, serve one another with whatever gift each of you has received. Whoever speaks must do so as one speaking the very words of God; whoever serves must do so with the strength that God supplies, so that God may be glorified in all things through Jesus Christ. To him belong the glory and the power for ever and ever. Amen' (1 Peter 4:10-11).

The Lutheran Council of Great Britain

History

Lutherans have worshipped in England for centuries, though rarely in English until about 40 years ago. The first official congregation was established in London in 1669 for Germans and Scandinavians. By the end of the 17th century, two further congregations (one German and one Scandinavian) had been established. Now there are Lutheran parishes and congregations in all parts of the country and Lutheran worship is conducted in a wide range of languages in Britain, reflecting Lutheranism's international character - Amharic, Cantonese, Danish, English, Estonian, Finnish, German, Hungarian, Icelandic, Latvian, Lithuanian, Mandarin, Norwegian, Polish, Swahili, Tigrinya, and Swedish. Together the various Lutheran churches in Britain minister to some 90,000 persons, mainly in languages other than English.

Worship

As Lutheran services have been developed over the centuries in many different cultures and countries, there are inevitably variations in expressions and styles of worship, which are reflected in Lutheran worship in Britain. Generally, Lutheran services are in the 'catholic' tradition, following the ancient liturgies and observing historic usage. Some congregations, however, offer a simpler style of worship. Crucifixes, candles and religious art are common.

In many Lutheran churches the priests or pastors wear traditional vestments, such as albs, stoles and chasubles. In other churches a black robe and ruff or bands are worn, often with a pectoral cross. Church buildings can be very ornate or rather simple, but always with the altar, pulpit and font as the main features. Differences in worship style or dress do not imply differences in theology or belief for Lutherans; often they have arisen for reasons of history or culture.

Music

Martin Luther extolled music as a 'precious gift of God', and said that music had been bestowed on humanity 'to remind them that they are created to praise and magnify the Lord.' Certainly from Luther's time onwards, music has always been an important part of Lutheran worship. The liturgies are often sung by the clergy and the congregation - it can happen that the sermon is virtually the only part of the service that is not sung. Hymns and instrumental music are common. Many traditional Lutheran hymns are unfamiliar (and seem a bit heavy) to most Christians in Britain, while others have entered the mainstream of British hymnody. Many of the older hymns are very long and strongly didactic, as they aimed at both beautifying the worship and instructing the congregation.

The musical aspect of Lutheran spirituality has given rise to much church music within Lutheranism. There have been many great Lutheran composers who wrote prolifically for their churches, such as Bach and Mendelssohn, and they still feature strongly in much Lutheran worship today.

Evangelical emphasis

The proclamation of the Word is fundamental in Lutheran worship. The word is 'evangelical' in the sense that the Gospel of Christ is at the centre of all proclamation, presented as God's gift of grace for us. For Lutherans 'evangelical' does not describe a type of churchmanship or piety or polity, but the promise character of the Word, which should be at the heart of all proclamation. All Lutherans would call themselves 'evangelical' in this sense, and it sometimes surprises other Christians to discover that these evangelicals might wear ornate vestments, use incense and refer to Holy Communion as the Mass.

Sacraments

'Evangelical' proclamation happens, or should happen, in all aspects of worship – hymns, liturgy, readings, sermons (which, in some cultures, are expected to be long and weighty) and in the celebration of the sacraments. Lutherans celebrate Holy Communion regularly, believing that Christ is really present in his fullness in the bread and wine of the sacrament, giving himself in his body and blood for the forgiveness of sins and spiritual nourishment. Usually communicants receive the wine from a common chalice, though in recent years individual cups have been used in some places. The bread is usually in wafer form and is put into the hand or placed into the communicant's mouth. Lutherans administer Holy Baptism to infants and adults, believing that God strengthens faith through the water used in this sacrament.

Renewal

As with most other churches, Lutheran congregations and parishes in Britain have been influenced in recent decades by liturgical or spiritual renewal movements in their home churches. Generally, there is now greater lay involvement in worship, which traditionally had been led only by the pastor. The language of services has been updated and musical settings and hymns offer many more styles and possibilities. There has also been a renewed interest in some older forms or practices that had been largely ignored, such as private confession, prayer candles, particular liturgies and pilgrimages.

The Methodist Church

Where, typically, do Methodists look for spiritual nourishment?

Means of grace

A classical response would be to look back to the method that provoked the nickname 'Methodists' for the brothers John and Charles Wesley and the other members of the 'Holy Club' in Oxford. From the late 1720s they rigorously followed a Rule of life that included regular attendance at Holy Communion, careful study of the Bible and other Christian texts, prison visiting and service of the poor, together with encouragement of each other in a strongly ethical life.

When the Methodist movement began and numerous Societies were formed (from 1739 onwards) there were *Rules for the Society* and the *Rules for a Helper* (a travelling preacher). These were constantly being developed during Wesley's lifetime.

In the *Rules* and in his preaching and teaching Wesley used the phrase 'means of grace' to describe the sources of spiritual nourishment and divided them into 'instituted means' and 'prudential means.' The former included private, family and public prayer, searching the scriptures 'which implies reading, hearing and meditating' and receiving the Lord's Supper at every opportunity, as well as fasting and 'Christian conference.'

The 'prudential means,' consisting mainly of meetings for fellowship, are a more distinctively Methodist contribution. An earnest Methodist would meet regularly in band, in class and in society. The bands were small selected groups of those seeking holiness. Those who joined a band were asked, 'Do you desire to be told of your faults, and that plain and home?' The phrase 'speaking in band' is still used occasionally of the bond of confidentiality that was attached to conversations in the band meeting. Every member of a society also belonged to a class. The aim of the class meeting, with the help of a class leader, was to grow in holiness: seeking 'perfect love.' The society meeting for fellowship combined worship and mutual encouragement.

There were other means of grace in early Methodism, most notably the hymns, but also the Lovefeast, the Watchnight and the Covenant Service. Wesley also believed that works of mercy, as well as works of piety, were means of grace. Field-preaching, the term Wesley used for preaching in the open air, also contributed to the distinctive ethos of Methodism and was undoubtedly a means of grace for the many who came to faith through it.

Do these traditional emphases still hold in the Methodist Church today? That question does not yield an easy answer. The two hundred and ten years since the death of Wesley have seen huge changes within Methodism, in its relationship to other Christian traditions, in its place in British society and in its local expression both in different parts of Britain and in different regions of the world.

Our roots

In nineteenth century England revivalist fervour and anti-authoritarian movements led to a number of splits. Towards the end of the century most of the branches of Methodism saw themselves as in effect Free Churches and identified themselves with the non-conformist conscience.

The British Methodist Church in its present form goes back to Methodist union in 1932. Since then it has been involved in the liturgical, theological and ecumenical changes and movements that have affected the life of most of the mainstream churches.

British Methodism was involved in the missionary movement from 1786 onwards and still has a strong sense of its place in the world church, expressed in the constitution of the Methodist Missionary Society, the membership of which is identical to that of the British Methodist Church:

> 'All members . . . . . have been regarded as called to share in the mission of the whole Church to offer Christ to every person in word, deed and corporate life.'

Today almost all the churches that began life because of British Methodist missionary work are either part of united churches or are autonomous Methodist churches. All over the world there are also United Methodist churches that are part of the American Methodist tradition. They also have a strong sense of connection with John Wesley but almost from the beginning have developed in different ways.

Modern emphases

Methodism in Britain in 2001 is hugely varied. A recent collection of essays by younger Methodists (*Methodism and the Future*, ed. Jane Craske and Clive Marsh, Cassell, 1999) did not deal explicitly with Methodist spirituality. It acknowledged indeed that 'spirituality' is not a very Methodist word and that in practice Methodists, like those of other faith traditions, often 'pick 'n mix' to find sustenance 'from many strands of knowledge and experience within and beyond the broad spectrum of Christian life and experience.' In drawing their spirituality from many sources modern Methodists are only doing what Wesley did in his *Christian Library*. That was an extraordinarily varied collection of selections and abridgements he produced for the early Methodists from patristic and puritan, Anglican and Roman Catholic writers together with lives of the reformers, Luther and Calvin.

An Anglican contributor to *Methodism and the Future,* Elizabeth Carnelly, testified to the strengths that drew her into a student Methodist Society as an undergraduate. They were the tradition of music and singing, the small cell group system, the commitment to living out faith each day and to mission, the lay-led nature of meetings and worship and the equality of women and men. In theory Methodists hold such resources as Charles Wesley's hymns, the Covenant Service, the *koinonia* of the small group, the importance of networking (which they describe as connexionalism), and a passionate commitment to both evangelism and dialogue in trust for the whole Church. In practice they do not always value them highly and of course they are not now unique to Methodists.

It is certainly no part of the Methodist way, however, to lock them up. We shall continue to say to others as Wesley said in his sermon, *Catholic Spirit*:

> 'Is your heart right, as my heart is with your heart?
> If it be, give me your hand.'

Holding different dimensions together

The special quality of Methodist spirituality does not lie in any single element within it. It is rather the deliberate holding together of dimensions that are often kept apart. It is both inward and outward, personal and corporate. As love for God grows, so too must love for people. It embraces different forms of prayer and worship: the ministry of the word and the ministry of the sacraments, liturgical prayer and the prayer of the heart, social concern and a sense of heaven.

The Moravian Church

The Church Year

Observance of the Church Year is a regular feature of the Moravian worship and there are customs and liturgies for each of the special seasons. The first Sunday in Advent is marked by the singing of the Hosanna Anthem, a musical setting of the words of welcome to Jesus as he came to Jerusalem, written by Christian Gregor in 1783. In most Moravian churches, the Advent Star will shine throughout the approach to Christmas.

On the Sunday before Christmas or on Christmas Eve, the Christingle is held. Originating in the Moravian Church, the first recorded service was in Marienborn in Germany in 1747 when each child present received a lighted candle decorated with a red ribbon to remind them of the birth of Christ 'who has kindled in each heart a flame which keeps ever burning to their joy and happiness'. The custom has become very widely used in churches in Britain in recent years, where children are given the gift of an orange holding a candle, representing Christ the Light of the world, and decorated with sweets, as a symbol of God's love freely offered to all in the incarnation. The traditional Christingle hymn begins:

> Morning Star, O cheering sight
> Ere Thou cam'st how dark earth's night.
> > Jesus mine,
> > In me shine,
> Fill my heart with light divine
> > (*Moravian Hymnbook* 45, v1)

Passion week and Easter are central to the Moravian perception of the purpose of Christ's life and there is a rich pattern of worship during this period. Each day during Passion Week congregations meet to read together a part of the story, the readings being interspersed with suitable hymns and prayers to help the worshippers meditate on the events recorded. On Maundy Thursday the reading is followed by a celebration of the Last Supper, and the reading continues on Good Friday with additional liturgical material provided. The climax to Moravian Easter worship comes early in the morning of Easter Day. As the minister enters the Church, he proclaims 'The Lord is Risen!' and the congregation responds 'He is risen, indeed!' and the celebration continues with the Easter Liturgy. For the second part of the service, where there is a congregational burial ground (in traditional Moravian usage 'God's Acre') the congregation moves outside to affirm again our resurrection faith and to remember the 'great cloud of witnesses', especially those of our own fellowship who have died during the year. The prayer includes the following:

> 'Keep us in unbroken fellowship with our brothers and sisters who in the past year have been called home and have entered into thy joy, and with the whole Church triumphant; that we may rejoice together in thy presence both now and evermore.'

The congregation will often return to the building to conclude the service with a celebration of Holy Communion, on this occasion, undoubtedly a 'Eucharist,' a great celebration of praise and thanksgiving. New liturgies have been provided for Whit-Sunday and Trinity in the 1960 edition. In many provinces, though not in Britain, liturgical forms are provided for Epiphany, Lent and Ascension.

The Moravian Church, then, may certainly be described as a liturgical church with a great variety of forms for regular Sunday worship and for the special days of the Christian year. It should be emphasized, however, that although liturgical worship is the norm, the Moravian Church has never required rigid conformity and does not wish to exclude other expressions of the faith. Special prayers for the day or relating to individuals are often inserted in the liturgy and there is provision for services with free forms of prayer.

Resources

An optional lectionary is provided for each Sunday, with Old Testament, Epistle and Gospel readings on a three year cycle, and is printed in the *Daily Watchwords* or *Moravian Textbook*, which is published in forty-one different languages and used by Christians of many denominations. For each day texts are provided from the Old and New Testaments, each text being illuminated by a hymn verse. *The Textbook* is used for private devotion but may also be used as a focus for congregational meditation. Especially is it the custom at a Lovefeast for the address to be based on the text for the day.

The Moravian Church contributed to the Evangelical Revival and thus shares similar concerns to Methodism and Evangelical Anglicanism. One of the shared concerns is great devotion to the person of Jesus, which has profoundly influenced the Moravian liturgy which has a number of prayers directed to Jesus.

Hymnody plays a major part in Moravian life, and is seen as of equal importance to the liturgy. Moravians are a singing people (as can be seen from the inclusion of set hymns and verses in the liturgy) and greatly value the *Moravian Hymnbook.*

Keeping the balance

Moravians maintain a balance between liturgical and spontaneous prayer. The attempt to preserve a balance between order and individual freedom in doctrine and in Christian living has always been a feature of Moravian life, expressed in the maxim: 'In essentials unity; in non-essentials liberty; in all things charity.' This concern is seen in the approach to worship as well as in other areas of the church's life.

The Moravian church provides an example of a reformed church that also values historic continuity with the church of the ages. Thus it has kept the three orders of ministers, bishop, presbyter and deacon. Elements of Catholic heritage are cherished, particularly in hymns. It has wedded these to a vibrant ecumenical and missionary vision. It is to be hoped that its role in church mission and unity can continue to flourish.

New Testament Assembly (NTA)

Spiritual Nourishment

New Testament Assembly subscribes to the biblical assertion that man is body, soul and spirit, and champions the view that these three parts need nurturing to enable the individual to be integrated and whole spiritually, physically and psychologically. This wholeness is deemed essential for members to relate effectively to God, themselves and others. This maturity is brought about by the Holy Spirit as He uses his ministering servants to give spiritual direction.

To provide spiritual nourishment an understanding of spirituality is paramount. Spirituality is the total matrix of beliefs, power, values and behaviours that shapes our consciousness, understanding, and capacity to relate to divine reality. It is a process by which we interpret, disclose, formulate, and adapt our understanding of God within specific context. There is affirmation and acknowledgment of God's all-pervasive presence, power and grace in every aspect of life and a strong inner conceptualised belief that He is ultimately in charge. This is lived out in many ways, the benchmark being our vibrant Sunday Morning Celebration Service.

Our spirituality, with God as its essence, underpins, shapes, informs, inspires and transforms our dealings with institutions, relationships, culture and cross-cultural situations and serves as a platform for empowerment, transformation, self-determination and autonomous living. It is sacrosanct, and venerable. Members are exhorted to aspire to worship an awesome God in 'spirit and in truth' - an expected outcome of all the activities we undertake.

Sunday Morning Celebration

Vibrant Sunday Morning Celebration Services are commonplace in all our congregations. They serve the purpose of corporate worship and adoration of an awesome God, which transcends spiritual, psychological, mental and physical being. It is an encounter with God that empowers and sustains. In addition, other objects are achieved, such as the reaffirming of persons and faith, the fostering of community solidarity, the maintenance of identity and the consolidating and reinforcing of structures which not only support, but form the springboard from which individuals are empowered to go out and be effective members of their local community in particular, and society in general.

Other sources of nourishment

Spiritual nourishment is provided by other means, including:

- **Prayer & intercessory meetings**—positively encourage the development of one's private prayer life as a means of soul nourishment.
- **Corporate & individual Bible studies**—a discipline greatly emphasised. The Word is life.
- **Healing services**—are usually attached to the Sunday Morning Celebration Service or some other service and concentrate on the healing of the whole person.
- **Fellowship meetings**—where stories are told, and strength and encouragement are received for the Christian journey.
- **Concerts**—much emphasis is placed on the release of soul energy in music, singing, dancing and high praise to God. There is often a cultural dimension to this worship.
- **Community activities**—through which members are encouraged to fulfil their social responsibilities.
- **Preaching and teaching**—with a great emphasis and instruction on holy living that is in line with the Holy Scriptures. The latter may take the form of seminars, discussion groups, quizzes, etc.
- **Pastoral care and counselling**—takes many forms, for example, personal and group care. In recent years formal training has been made available to those who feel called to the ministry of Christian Counselling and Care.
- **Formal Theological training**—at the Institute of Christian Training.
- **Celebration of the Lord's Supper**.

- **Family gatherings**—provide the vehicle for the cross fertilisation and transmission of spiritual and family values. They also serve as a means of passing on the family legacy, whatever that is.
- **Youth forums and retreats**—discovery and use of ministry gifts, talents and potential, as well as the affirming of individuals.
- **Impartation of survival skills**—practical, spiritual and social, for example, child rearing, relational and people skills.
- **Cell groups**—providing for the development of individuals in a more personal and close-knit environment.
- **Mentoring**—professional as well as on an ad hoc basis as necessary, to determine spiritual direction.

The work of God

Central to our spirituality is the belief that God, through the aegis of the Holy Spirit, is at work binding, healing, nurturing, sustaining and liberating relationships. This is demonstrated by touching and hugging which acknowledges the humanity of the person, embracing which affirms the person, the sharing of good and not-so-good stories, hopes, aspirations—to empathise, feel with and experience each other's pain and successes. Above all is the feeling of solidarity, significance, and worthiness. A side-effect is the moulding of character and personality development, another being the release of pent-up emotions, tension and stress which would otherwise paralyse and render individuals impotent in their daily lives.

New Testament Assembly firmly believes that every member has been given a gift or gifts by God for specific outworking in the building of the Kingdom, and has therefore created opportunities for individuals to utilise their gifts and become actualised and fulfilled. Formally this is known as 'Body Ministry' or 'The Priesthood of all Believers', and *Welcome to Your Ministry* - a booklet outlining this principle was produced in 1997. Believers are encouraged to seek God's plan for their life and to follow closely his leading and bidding in order to be Christ-actualised. Striving for the spiritual gifts recorded in *Ephesians* is an aspiration of all believers.

Another important function of New Testament Assembly is the interpretation and translation of systems, culture, legislation for our people, thereby effecting desirable attitudes and enabling our members to live within given parameters whilst responsibly exercising their freedom.

As the Church attracts the second and third generation of African and Caribbean families a radical appraisal of the modes of delivery of spiritual nourishment is taking place. Fundamental doctrines have not changed but our mind-sets have. Facilitating the needs, and incorporating the thinking and attitudes of generation X is a challenge. This process and journey is sometimes painful, nevertheless it is one which is worthwhile pursuing. Already it has added new dimensions to our churches and has diversified our worship.

The Council of Oriental Orthodox Christian Churches (COOCC)

The Oriental Orthodox Churches are, listed alphabetically, Armenian, Coptic, Eritrean, Ethiopian, Syrian, and Syro-Indian Orthodox Churches.

The spiritual nourishment of our churches is drawn from the early Christian spiritual heritage of Jerusalem, Alexandria, the see of St Mark, and Antioch, the first see of St. Peter, the almost forgotten cradle of Christianity where 'the disciples were first called Christian', (Acts 11:26). The spiritual heritage, initially developed in Palestine and Mesopotamia, was subsequently adopted and integrated by the nations of the Old World, in the early centuries of the spread of Christianity. Oriental Orthodox Churches are Apostolic Churches of the Word and the Sacrament. The faithful, regardless of their denominations, derive their daily spiritual nourishment from the following:

The Bible

The Scriptures are the Alpha and Omega of our spiritual nourishment, and every member of the faithful should have ready access to the Bible at all times. Uniquely, the Bible in our Churches is placed on the lectern in front of the altar, 24 hours a day all through the year, not only during the Mass, so the faithful can read the Word of the Lord and be blessed continuously.

Sacraments

The Sacraments are central to our life, worship and spirituality. Our Churches believe in seven sacraments: Baptism, Confirmation, Penance, Holy Eucharist, Matrimony, Holy Orders and Unction, or order of the sick. They correspond and relate to all stages of our life. The celebration of each Sacrament is immensely spiritually uplifting and reviving through which the souls of the people taking part derive spiritual strength and grace.

The Sacred Liturgy

Together with the Bible, the sacred Liturgy managed to sow the seed of faith and establish solid roots to sustain the growth of Christianity over two thousand years. Oriental Orthodox 'continued steadfastly in the apostles' doctrine and fellowship, and in breaking of bread' (Acts 2:42). They adopted many liturgies, the Liturgy of St. James, the brother of the Lord, being the oldest and most popular among them. It was written in the Syriac language which was spoken in Galilee when Jesus taught there, and became the language of the church of the East, as far as India and China and nations along the Nile Valley. Liturgies were written specially to celebrate each sacrament and other ecclesiastical events: 'do that in remembrance of me' (Luke 22:19). The Liturgy for the Holy Eucharist is central to our Church life '..if you don't eat the flesh of the Son of man and drink his blood, you have no life in you' (John 6:53-54). The Holy Communion is a daily source of spiritual nourishment for our faithful and a necessity for salvation, 'Now you are the body of Christ and individual members of it' (1 Corinthians 12:27).

Music

The Apostle Paul indicates in his epistles that praise, psalms and spiritual songs accompanied worship in church, and were an important part of its spiritual life. 'Be filled with the spirit, addressing one another in psalms and hymns and spiritual songs, singing and making melody to the Lord with all your heart, always and for everything giving thanks in the name of our Lord Jesus Christ to God the Father' (Ephesians 5:18-20). The theme was repeated to the Colossians, 'Let the word of Christ dwell in you richly, as you teach and admonish one another in all wisdom, and as you sing psalms and hymns and spiritual songs with thankfulness in your hearts to God' (Colossians 3:16). Music as a vehicle for spiritual enhancement is shown in Psalms, Proverbs, and Lamentations of Jeremiah. This is still the way the faithful spiritually approach their creator through music. 'O sing to the Lord a new song; sing to the Lord, all the earth! Sing to the Lord, bless his name; tell of his salvation from day to day' (Psalms 96:1-2). 'The Lord is at hand to save me; so let the music of our praises resound all over our life long in the house of the Lord' (Isaiah 38:20).

Teaching of the Church Fathers

The exegesis and teaching of our Church Fathers have kept the light of the scripture shining through the darkest of ages, encouraging godly living and martyrdom. 'It is through many persecutions that we must enter the kingdom of God' (Acts 14:22). These persecutions were merely caused by being Christian, 'Persecution will indeed come to everyone who wants to live a godly life as a follower of Christ Jesus' (2 Timothy 3:12). Through their spiritual teaching, many of the Church Fathers had earned high esteem through out the Christendom. The poems of St. Ephrem the Syrian spiritually nourished generations and still do.

Fasting

Fasting as spiritual self-control was first introduced to Adam at the Garden of Eden, 'The Lord God commanded the first man, saying, "of every tree of the garden you may freely eat: but of the tree of the knowledge of good and evil, you shall not eat of it"' (Genesis 2:17). The Old Testament tell us of the effect of fasting on spiritual well-being (Exodus 34:28; Daniel 1:2-3,8-17; Isaiah 58:6-7; Jonah 3:1-10). To show the spiritual power of fasting and teach us to fast, our Lord Jesus Christ fasted for forty days and nights (Luke 4:1-2). The combination of fasting and praying seem to be the best spiritual weapon to enable us to face our spiritual enemy the Devil and perpetual temptation. Our churches organise fasting so the faithful can be spiritually nourished.

Feasts

Christmas and Easter are a time of spiritual exhilaration during which the faithful relive the life of Jesus, his birth, suffering, passion, death on the cross and resurrection, 'For me to live is Christ' (Philippians

1:21). These with the feasts of the Virgin Mary, with other remembrances and celebration throughout the year, are the pit-stops of our spiritual life.

Pilgrimage

Our churches are committed to pilgrimage to the Church of the Resurrection (the Holy Sepulchre) in Jerusalem, and other Biblical sites in the Holy Land. Sadly, the majority of our faithful in the Middle East have been denied the right to enjoy this spiritual zenith for the last four decades. Many lived and died without the fulfilment of this spiritual pledge. Shrines of the Saints and Church Fathers, and ancient monasteries are important places of pilgrimage for our faithful, who visit them regularly to celebrate a feast, baptise children, make a spiritual retreat, enjoy monastic life or just to be blessed.

Prayers

In today's secular environment, the busy and stressful daily schedule and life-style of many of our faithful may not allow them to participate in the sacred liturgy, so prayerful life is for many the only spiritual consolation. It is an integral and essential source for the daily spiritual nourishment. Our spiritual heritage contains prayers, intercessions and supplications for all human daily needs and occasions, to 'pray without ceasing' (1 Thessalonians 5:16). Finally our sisters and brothers, 'If you have faith, everything you ask for in prayer, you will receive' (Matthew 21:22), for the sake of Jesus' passion for unity, let us pray as Churches Together, 'the Our Father', in the Syriac version, which was prayed by our Lord Jesus Christ, in his mother tongue:

+ABUN DBACHMAYO, NIZC ADACH SCHMOJ, TICE MALCUTHO, NEHBE SOBYONO, AYCANO DBACHMAYO, OF BARGO GABLAN, LAHMO SUN KONAN, YAUMONO SCHBUDLAN, HAUBAY WAHTO HAIN, AYCANO DOF HANAN, ECHBAKEN EL HAYOBEIN, LO TA'ALAM NOSIUNO, ELO FASOLA, MEN BISCHO METUL, DI LOJ HE MALCUZO, HAILO TUSCHBUHTO, LOLAM, OLMIN. AMIN

Religious Society of Friends in Britain (Quakers)

'It is in the **corporate** practice of predominantly silent worship that the distinctive characteristic of Quaker worship is found, and the word 'corporate' has to be stressed so that this silent worship may be distinguished from the silence of Trappist monks or of Carthusians, each in his own cell.' (Horton Davies, *Worship and Theology in England.* 1966, Vol 6, p 403.)

Such a form of worship requires rich sources of spiritual nourishment if it is to sustain the worshippers and this poses a constant challenge. The Bible has always held a central place but even the first generation of Friends believed that what they often called the Inward Light of Christ is available to all, whether or not they have any knowledge of the Bible or the gospel narrative. From the 1650s George Fox's mission was to call people to turn to their Inward Teacher, the Living Christ, and wait to receive his word unmediated by priest, minister or sacrament. He asserted 'Christ is come to teach his people himself'.

Resources

An important resource is the book in which the Yearly Meeting of Friends in Britain collects significant passages which express its members' experience over three centuries. This is revised by every generation of Friends, the last revision in 1994 changing the previous title, *Christian Faith and Practice in the Experience of the Society of Friends* to *Quaker Faith and Practice: A Book of Christian Discipline (QFP).* In an attempt to emphasise the unity of faith and life, the book now incorporates in one volume both an anthology of passages in which this wisdom is expressed and the regulations and structures by which we conduct our business. Its contents are arranged in twenty-nine sections under headings such as *Approaches to God - worship and prayer, Caring for one another, Openings, Close relationships, Our peace testimony, Reflections, Unity and diversity* and *Leadings.*

The corporate wisdom from this collection is distilled in *Advices and Queries* with which the book opens - also published separately in a small booklet. Their origins lie in a series of formal queries addressed to local Meetings which required written answers. In this form they covered a range of factual and spiritual matters from the statistics of membership to the subjective, 'How doth the Truth prosper among you?' Their function today is described thus:

'The advices and queries are intended for use in our meetings, for private devotion and reflection, as a challenge and inspiration to us as Friends in our personal lives and in our life as a religious community, and as a concise expression of our faith and practice readily available to enquirers and to the wider world.' *(QFP 1. 05)*

They are introduced by the words:

'As Friends we commit ourselves to a way of worship which allows God to teach and transform us. We have found corporately that the Spirit, if rightly followed, will lead us into truth, unity and love: all our testimonies grow from this leading.' *(QFP 1. 01)*

The first two *Advices and Queries* build on this experience as follows:

'Take heed, dear Friends, to the promptings of love and truth in your hearts. Trust them as the readings of God whose Light shows us our darkness and brings us to new life.

'Bring the whole of your life under the ordering of the spirit of Christ. Are you open to the healing power of God's love? Cherish that of God within you, so that this love may grow in you and guide you. Let your worship and your daily life enrich each other. Treasure your experience of God, however it comes to you. Remember that Christianity is not a notion but a way.' *(QFP 1. 02)*

As the Society emerged from an enclosed culture around 1900, London Yearly Meeting (now Britain Yearly Meeting) moved towards an ever more liberal and inclusive stance, eventually admitting into membership even people of other faiths who felt at home in the silence of a worshipping community in which specific doctrines and beliefs were irrelevant to the corporate experience of transcendence.

Incarnated spirituality

But how can such a nebulous spirituality be nourished? Friends have struggled to answer this question satisfactorily and, just as those in the nineteenth century tempered the distinctive Quaker experience by absorbing the evangelical theology of the day, Friends today seek enrichment in sources as diverse as the arts (a definite taboo for almost three centuries), Celtic Christianity, creation spirituality, eastern mysticism, ecumenical resources, inspiration from other faiths, Ignatian meditation, retreats and the writing of spiritual journals. Whereas the resources of art and music, creative and spiritual writings from many sources are now enthusiastically embraced - 'Are you open to new light from whatever source it may come?' (from *Advices and Queries* 7), Friends would still affirm the message of Fox and his companions that a spirituality based on silent seeking and expressed in service to the world is indeed viable. It might be said that Quakerism is rooted in an incarnated spirituality.

Meeting for worship

In the silence of meeting for worship, Friends gather to open themselves to the guidance of the Holy Spirit. One or more of those present may be moved to spoken ministry. The Society's spiritual health and the right holding of meetings for worship are the particular concern of 'elders' who are appointed for three-year periods by each group of local meetings. Among their responsibilities are:

'to meet regularly to uphold the meeting and its members in prayer; to guide those who share in our meetings towards a deeper experience of worship; to encourage preparation of mind and spirit, and study of the Bible and other writings that are spiritually helpful...' *(QFP 12.12 a)*

Surveys of Friends in Britain show that the meeting for worship is a major source of spiritual nurture. 'An hour of silence in the presence of other Friends brings peace inwardly and a feeling of the nearness of God.' Meeting for worship may bring comfort and consolation: 'Meeting provides an atmosphere of peace and devotion in which to dwell on all that is positive'. There is a recognition that it may also challenge and disturb, for the essence of spiritual life is transformation. For Fox the Inward Light was more than a metaphor and the spiritual discipline which he taught is summarised in the words:

'The first step to peace is to stand still in the Light... for power and strength to stand against that nature which the Light discovers; for here grace grows, here is God alone glorified and exalted, and the unknown truth, unknown to the world, made manifest.'

The practice of this discipline has been an important source of spiritual regeneration over the past few years, uniting as it does the mystical, the prophetic and the practical to foster an attitude in which social concern is a natural outcome of the inspiration to build the Kingdom. The social testimonies in which this is expressed are the evidence of the 'incarnated spirituality' mentioned earlier: they take the place of doctrinal beliefs in other traditions and lead to what has also been called a 'practical mysticism' which is unique to the Society of Friends.

The Roman Catholic Church

The Sacred Liturgy

Sacrosanctum Concilium (SC), the Second Vatican Council's Constitution on the Sacred Liturgy (4 December 1963), makes it clear that, for Roman Catholics, Christ encountered in the Sacred Liturgy is the primary source of spiritual nourishment. 'It is the liturgy through which, especially in the divine sacrifice of the Eucharist, 'the work of our redemption is accomplished', and it is through the liturgy, especially, that the faithful are enabled to express in their lives and manifest to others the mystery of Christ and the real nature of the true Church... The liturgy daily builds up those who are in the Church, making of them a holy temple of the Lord, a dwelling place for God in the Spirit, to the mature measure of the fullness of Christ. At the same time it marvellously increases their power to preach Christ and thus show forth the Church, a sign lifted up among the nations...' (SC 2).

All the other elements of spiritual nourishment are seen to flow from this central understanding and it is the presence and action of Christ, in the power of the Holy Spirit, mediating between humanity and the Father, which makes them effective. Even so 'the liturgy does not exhaust the entire activity of the Church' (SC9).

'To accomplish so great a work Christ is always present in his Church, especially in her liturgical celebrations. He is present in the sacrifice of the Mass not only in the person of his minister, 'the same now offering through the ministry of priests, who formerly offered himself on the cross', but especially in the eucharistic species. By his power he is present in the sacraments so that when anybody baptises it is really Christ himself who baptises. He is present in the word since it is he himself who speaks when the holy scriptures are read in the Church. Lastly he is present when the Church prays and sings, for he has promised 'where two or three are gathered together in my name there am I in the midst of them' (Matthew 18:20). Every liturgical celebration, because it is an action of Christ the Priest and of his Body, which is the Church, is a sacred action surpassing all others.

No other action of the Church can equal its efficacy by the same title and to the same degree' (SC 7).

Only when these fundamental principles are established can we list the various elements of spiritual nourishment. Two further points need to be borne in mind. There is an intrinsic inter-relationship in sacramental worship between Word and Sacramental signs. It was to emphasise this that Vatican II wished to restore the Scripture to a more prominent place in the liturgy. 'Sacred scripture is of the greatest importance in the celebration of the liturgy. For it is from it that lessons are read and explained in the homily, and psalms are sung. It is from the scriptures that the prayers, collects and hymns draw their inspiration and their force, and that actions and signs derive their meaning' (SC 7).

Eucharist

The Church's most important communal act of worship is the Eucharist. 'Taking part in the eucharistic sacrifice, the source and summit of the Christian life, (the faithful) offer the divine victim to God and themselves along with it. And so it is that, both in the offering and in Holy Communion, each in his own way... has his own part to play in the liturgical action. Then, strengthened by the body of Christ in the eucharistic communion, they manifest in a concrete way that unity of the People of God which this holy sacrament aptly signifies and admirably realises' (*Lumen Gentium* 11). For the significance of the Eucharist see *One Bread One Body* (Catholic Bishops' Conferences of England & Wales, Scotland & Ireland, 1999).

Celebrating the Eucharist impels us towards involvement in issues of justice and peace: 'the renewal in the Eucharist of the covenant between the Lord and his people draws the faithful into the compelling love of Christ and sets them on fire' (SC10).

In practice the Roman Catholic Church distinguishes between worship **in** the Eucharist (the sacramental, liturgical action) and worship **of** the Eucharist as a permanent sacrament. Roman Catholics are nourished by prayer before the Blessed Sacrament (ie in the presence of the reserved Eucharist). Public adoration of the Incarnate Word in the Eucharist is encouraged and provided for in a number of para-liturgies and devotional rites, such as Exposition of the Blessed Sacrament.

Holy Communion (from a recent Mass or the reserved Sacrament) is taken to the sick at home or in hospital. Holy Communion is administered to the dying (when it is known as Viaticum).

Sacraments

In the Roman Catholic Church the Sacraments are Baptism, Confirmation, Eucharist, Penance, Anointing of the Sick, Marriage and Holy Orders. 'The purpose of the sacraments is to sanctify the faithful, to build up the Body of Christ, and finally, to give worship to God. Because they are signs they also instruct. They not only presume faith, but by words and objects they also nourish, strengthen and express it. They do, indeed, confer grace, but in addition, the very act of celebrating them most effectively disposes the faithful to receive this grace to their profit, to worship God duly, and to practice charity' (SC 59).

Sacramentals, such as Palm branches, ashes, and holy water, are common aids to prayer and devotion, and 'are sacred signs which bear a resemblance to the sacraments. They signify effects, particularly of a spiritual nature, which are obtained through the Church's intercession. By them the faithful are disposed to receive the chief effects of the sacraments and various occasions in life rendered holy' (SC 60) . Their usage and popularity outside the liturgy may vary.

Prayer: communal and personal

'The spiritual life, however, is not limited solely to participation in the liturgy. The Christian is indeed called to pray with others, but he must also enter into his bedroom to pray to his Father in secret; furthermore, according to the teaching of the apostle, he must pray without ceasing' (SC 12). Lectio Divina, Spiritual Direction and Retreats are significant ways of deepening the life of prayer.

Private prayer and reflection are encouraged within the liturgy by providing periods of silence. 'Meaningful silence is an element in celebration which must be given its due place… In the Penitential Act and the pause before the Collect the people should turn their thoughts within themselves; after the readings and the homily they should meditate on what they have heard; after the communion they should praise God and pray in their hearts.' (General Instruction on the Roman Missal 23.)

The Prayer of the Church, or Divine Office, holds first place in public, non-sacramental worship and has been growing in usage and popularity in parishes which do not have the religious or monastic tradition. 'The Church, by celebrating the Eucharist and by other means, especially the celebration of the Divine Office, is ceaselessly engaged in praising the Lord and interceding for the salvation of the entire world. The Divine Office, in keeping with ancient Christian tradition, is so devised that the whole course of the day and night is made holy by the praise of God' (SC 83/84).

The Liturgical Year with its great Seasons and Feasts informs and encourages the spiritual development of individuals and the community. Advent and Christmas, Lent and Easter focus on distinctive aspects of the mystery of salvation. Growth in the observance of the Easter Triduum, RCIA (Rite of Christian Initiation for Adults) and adult baptisms, and in understanding Easter as the fulcrum of the Church's year have been important post-Vatican II developments.

The Veneration of Our Lady and the Saints (SC 111) the use of Sacred Music (SC 112-121) and Art (SC 122-129) are all important elements in spiritual nourishment, though properly taking a secondary place in terms of importance.

Distinctive elements

Much more could be said of the other distinctive elements simply listed here: devotional objects (rosary, medals, scapulars, statues), veneration of relics, popular devotions (Stations of the Cross, the Rosary, Novenas), pilgrimages (Holy Land, Rome, Lourdes, Fatima, Taizé, Santiago, Walsingham, Holywell, Aylesford), and the granting of Indulgences. Many of these have changed in their application and use during the last 40 years, but all are to be found among Roman Catholic spiritual practices.

Many Roman Catholics are nourished spiritually by the sense of universal communion between the living and the faithful departed (prayer and Masses for the dead). The practice of requesting Mass intentions is common in parishes and understood as a particular way of associating with the Eucharistic Sacrifice, when prayer is offered for a particular person.

Awareness of their Communion with the See of Peter also nourishes the spiritual lives of many individuals, families and communities. Papal or Apostolic Blessings are often obtained to mark parish, wedding or ordination jubilees. Prayer in union 'with Peter and the apostles' is experienced in this way and a sense of universal communion deepened.

Various complementary Schools of Prayer have been initiated by or around charismatic individuals; chief among these 'spiritualities' are the Benedictine, Franciscan, Dominican, Carmelite and Ignatian traditions. Often individuals adopt a way of life and prayer associated with a religious order as oblates or tertiaries.

Charismatic Renewal has led to a new experience of communal, informal prayer for Roman Catholics, encouraging prayerful use of the Scriptures and ecumenical openness. The growth of local Prayer Groups has been of major significance in parish life, especially those whose focus is reflection on the Scripture.

The Russian Orthodox Church

Holy Tradition

The Orthodox Church has as its head the Lord Jesus Christ and celebrates its birth at Pentecost, with the coming of the Holy Spirit, who has remained at its heart ever since. This understanding of the indwelling of the Holy Spirit, not only in individuals but also in the Church itself, is central to our understanding of our spiritual life.

Spiritual nourishment in the Orthodox Church is realised through our embodiment in Holy Tradition: the life in the Holy Spirit as handed on to us from the Early Church. This includes, among other elements, Scripture, the Creed, the sacraments, the services, prayers and music, monasticism, the writings of the Fathers, the Church canons and the rules of fasting and feasting, icons and iconography and the practice of spiritual fatherhood and motherhood.

Tradition is a wholeness of our faith. Spirituality is not an optional extra, divorced from everyday Christian life, but a natural and integral part of it. The person, body and soul, is sanctified through the sacraments; time is sanctified in the feasts and fasts of the Church year, whose focus and crown is Easter, the Feast of Feasts, when we celebrate the unbounded joy of the bodily Resurrection of Christ. This is the central truth around which our whole life revolves.

Places, such as churches and our homes, and material objects such as icons, are sanctified with blessings. Thus everything in life is brought within the experience of our Christian faith and nourishes it.

Worship

Distinctively Orthodox is our life in worship, which is a foretaste of Heaven on earth. This is particularly true of the Divine Liturgy (the Eucharist) where by the power of the Holy Spirit the bread and wine becomes the Body and Blood of Christ and we participate incipiently in the Kingdom. This is the prime nourishment that Christ has ordained for his flock, to make us living members of his Body at work in the world today.

Our other sacraments, such as baptism, chrismation, confession, marriage, ordination and the anointing of the sick, are similarly accomplished by the Holy Spirit who acts through material means to fill us with divine grace and make God's love present to us.

Our service texts are contained in a great number of volumes of words and music. In these words the theology of the Church is expressed and available to all; the music (our services being sung or chanted throughout) conveys feelings beyond words. We also enter into worship with all our senses, by using incense, making gestures and seeing the icons, vestments and church architecture that all convey their own deep meaning. The human person is recognised as a unique being of body and soul together, both redeemed by Christ; therefore the whole person worships and lives the Christian life.

Icons in particular are not religious art but sacred art, a sign that in the Incarnation matter can be pervaded by spirit and can become a focus of Presence. They also remind us that the whole Church is gathered in one for worship by portraying Christ, the saints and the angels who are otherwise invisibly present with us.

Monasticism

Monasticism plays an important part in Orthodox life. Monasteries are often places of joyful pilgrimage. Most of our services were developed in the monastic communities, and the practice of being nurtured by a spiritual father also originated in the monasteries and is now a feature of the lives of Orthodox lay people as well. This personal spiritual direction, together with the sacrament of Confession, ensures that each person grows up within the free discipline of the Christian community, knowing he/she is accepted and loved despite their sins.

There is a large corpus of Orthodox prayers, including books of daily prayers that enable all Orthodox to be part of one body of prayer even when physically alone. Specifically Orthodox is the use of the Jesus Prayer: 'Lord Jesus Christ, Son of God, have mercy on me a sinner'. This prayer, again monastic in origin, is also used by lay people and can be the foundation of a person's prayer life, repeated perhaps more or less continuously (but *always* with total concentration on the meaning of the words) during the day, or perhaps only at certain times.   It can be attuned to a person's breathing and heartbeat, although these physical exercises are not a necessity: its essence is always the genuine cry to the Lord of this 'prayer of the heart'.

Another practice, deriving from the Early Church and developed in the monasteries, is that of fasting: when on most Wednesdays and Fridays and during the fasting seasons such as Lent and Advent, we truly learn that spiritual and physical nourishment are part of God's total care for us. This is also true of our equal emphasis on celebrating the feasts of the Church.

The writings of the Fathers, from the simple Desert Fathers of Egypt to the theology of the Cappadocian Fathers, the *Philokalia,* the Russian *startsi* (spiritual elders) of the nineteenth century to modern Greek, Russian and other spiritual writers, to name a few examples, afford a vast body of texts which can deepen and encourage the life in Christ.

The Church as one

Because Orthodox are aware of dying to Christ and being reborn in Him at baptism, we perceive the Church as one in heaven and on earth, and we are therefore free to ask the prayers and support of the saints and other departed Christians just as we would any other living friend. This familiarity with the saints, and the desire to follow the examples of their lives, is another way we are nourished in the Christian life.

In our Russian Diocese of Sourozh in Britain we specifically nourish our members through an annual residential Conference; a summer

Children's Camp; a Diocesan Assembly; a Diocesan Patronal Liturgy; publications (the Cathedral newsletter and our journal *Sourozh)* and pilgrimages. Individual parishes organise talks, study groups, Sunday Schools and a range of groups and activities to cater for their needs. We call our priests 'Father' (followed by their Christian name) and the church community is very much a familial one in which we are nourished as members of the one Body of the Lord Jesus Christ in order to bring his light to the world.

The Salvation Army

Salvationists are nourished by the reality of Salvationism as a worldwide fellowship extending to over one hundred countries.

Personal experience

Initial awareness of personal Christian conversion is the basis of membership. The Grace of Jesus elicits our love to Him and love becomes the personal dynamic of life and service. Personal experience and mission are integrated and sustained by the fellowship of worship. There is a personal and communal intention to embark upon living in those terms perceived within the word of God. Having said that, there is always the Protestant dilemma faced in the strength and weakness of the priesthood of all believers. Differing emphases gather about the eleven articles of Salvationism.

Worship

Salvationists are nourished by the worldwide mission in which worship embraces all cultures and national expressions. The crucified, risen and glorified Jesus is the centre of all worship from conservative to charismatic. As Jesus promised, the Holy Spirit takes the things that belong to Jesus and reveals them in the person and the fellowship. We sing the ancient song of creation to its Creator; we sing the new song of the redeemed to the Redeemer.

The Word of God in both Old and New Testaments nourishes Salvationists - both the one and the many. While there are no formal sacraments (as is the case with the Religious Society of Friends) there is a freedom to celebrate the real presence of Jesus at all meals and in all meetings - just as Jesus and His friends shared together in fellowship meals. Thus the sacrificial love of Jesus is the rationale for Lovefeasts and the hallowing of all meals in home and church.

The pragmatism of Salvationism insists upon no separation between the sacred and the secular. Yet within each Salvation Army centre the

Mercy Seat or Penitent Form has profound significance. This provides a means of grace. This is a place of personal communion with the living Lord Jesus. This central reality of the Mercy Seat is a worldwide phenomenon.

Generally speaking, at each centre of worship, each Sunday there are two meetings styled Holiness and Salvation/Gospel. In themselves many would see these meetings as nourishing an ongoing tradition, as all manner of prayer is shared, and spiritual hopes identified, as well as that sense of communion in being with Jesus and his friends. General John Gowans reiterates central features of nourishment for the Salvation Army. He includes the saving of souls; the blessing of his people, service to the community from local to worldwide. He also affirms the Bible, the Mercy Seat, and the Salvation Army flag, for its tricolor points to Trinity.

Holiness

The pragmatic nature of Salvationism insists that the real presence of Jesus may be celebrated in the market place, home or worship centre, and indeed anywhere. For the Lord Jesus Christ is the one true sacrament of God for a Salvationist. His incarnation and continuing gracious presence with his people by means of the indwelling Holy Spirit remains the tremendous fascination of our faith. The redeemed community eat and drink together as they remember the broken body and outpoured blood of the Lord Jesus. The Lovefeast of faith anticipates the feasts of eternity. The concept is expressed in verse:

> 'My life must be Christ's broken bread
> My love his outpoured wine
> A cup o'erfilled, a table spread
> Beneath His name and sign;
> That other souls refreshed and fed
> May share His life through mine.'

All that we seek to do in life and service is in remembrance of his dying love and resurrection power as we are enabled by the Holy

Spirit.   He nourishes the soldiers, adherents and friends of the Salvation Army.   From its inception, Salvationists have had opportunity to pray or testify in meetings both indoor and out of doors. Simply stated, God speaks through his Word and we speak to God in prayer. This promotes a lifestyle of simplicity, trust and thankfulness.

Internationally, the worldwide fellowship makes it possible for a Holiness doctrine to become a way of life, involving the personal, relational, social and political, as they occur in cross-cultural contexts. The individual is encouraged and enthused by the immediate group and all the Salvationist world. This, more than ever before, moves beyond this one denomination to embrace the whole Christian community as it is and as it will yet become.

The United Reformed Church

Worship

Spiritual nourishment comes primarily from meeting with the local church in Sunday worship. The core of worship is the reading and preaching of the Word of God in the Scriptures, and the celebration of the gospel sacraments. These are the primary means of grace.

Prayer is another essential element in public worship. Whilst the practice of extempore prayer is not as common as it was, the language of prayer should be comprehensible, relevant and yet capable of taking the worshipper into the presence of God. With that general observation, no particular form or order of prayer is prescribed. Some leaders use set prayers, some write their own.

Our tradition is very much that of singing our faith, so we are nourished by everything from metrical psalms and the hymns of Doddridge and Watts to the hymns of Kaan and Wren. Many of us sing from ecumenical sources , including those of Iona and Taizé.

The United Reformed Church recognises the ancient ecumenical creeds as well as the statements of faith made in its own tradition from time to time. For some these are sources of spiritual nourishment, either in public worship or private devotion.

Symbol and silence are more recent discoveries for us, but increasingly people are nourished by them. A small but growing number appreciate retreats.

Spiritual nourishment

Because so much emphasis is placed on the Word of God (see Basis of Union of the United Reformed Church, paragraph 12), groups for Bible study or for the discussion of faith and life issues are often part of our congregational life. From time to time the Church provides material to help such groups. It would be false to claim that anything like a majority attend these groups, but those who do should be nourished by them.

The structure of the United Reformed Church has two features which are particularly significant in spiritual nourishment. One is the network of pastoral care - the responsibility of the elders' meeting— through which every person should receive care and oversight. Thus faith and fellowship are related to both the ordinary and the significant moments of personal life. The other is the opportunity for every member to participate in the local church meeting, and to seek with others of varying perceptions what God may be saying to and requiring of his people. This shared discipline is very significant for us.

For the past 200 years members of the United Reformed Church and its constituent traditions have been nourished by a dynamic contact with the world church and its various spiritual expressions. The nature of that contact has changed radically in the last 25 years. It is now more mutual and (because travel is easier) more direct. The increasingly diverse ethnic composition of the church's membership opens us even more easily to a variety of spiritualities.

What has been written in the last paragraph applies equally to our drawing on the spirituality of other Christian traditions in the last 100 years. We also have been affected by the liturgical movement and renewal movement and so it is easy to drink living water from the springs of other traditions.

Engagement

Another part of our tradition is that of engagement with the life of the local community, and with the political and social concerns of the country. In the past 50 years or so that has developed into world concerns and particularly the area of development. A concern to oppose injustice and to meet the needs of the poor provides a deep source for much of our spirituality.

Last but not least we would testify to personal discipleship of Jesus Christ as a rich source of spiritual nourishment. Whilst we put a great deal of emphasis on fellowship in worship and in our life, that is not to deny that every believer has access to the throne of grace. For many that is where nourishment begins.

'The United Reformed Church and the purpose of the Church

Within the one, holy, catholic, apostolic Church the United Reformed Church acknowledges its responsibility under God:

- to make its life a continual offering of itself and the world to God in adoration and worship through Jesus Christ;

- to receive and express the renewing life of the Holy Spirit in each place and in its total fellowship, and there to declare the reconciling and saving power of the life, death and resurrection of Jesus Christ;

- to live out, in joyful and sacrificial service to all in their various physical and spiritual needs, that ministry of caring, forgiving and healing love which Jesus Christ brought to all whom he met;

- and to bear witness to Christ's rule over the nations in all the variety of their organised life'.

The Basis of Union of the United Reformed Church (paragraph 11)
Adopted 1972

The Countess of Huntingdon's Connexion

The Connexion is currently a group of 23 independent churches. The property and the appointment of ministers is overseen by a Trustee Board but the leadership of each church is in the hands of the Pastor and the leadership team, however called. In the light of this it is difficult to generalise or to say that we have any 'unique' expression of spirituality.

Evangelical

All the churches could be classed as 'evangelical'. The Connexion and some individual churches are members of the Evangelical Alliance. Bearing this in mind the main source of nourishment will be the reading, study and application of the written 'Word of God'. Preaching from the scriptures will form a major part of any worship service. Most churches will have some form of midweek Bible study or fellowship group and at the moment a number are using the Alpha course as a means of spiritual input and evangelism.

Worship

Praise and worship are expressed in both traditional and modern styles. Many churches will give opportunity for open worship and prayer during a service. Holy Communion will be observed once or twice a month. Although the Articles of Faith mention paedo-baptism, this will be only very occasionally practised, the vast majority of baptisms are Believers' Baptism by immersion. Prayer in its varying forms will be part of each church programme. In the main, its emphasis would be intercessory. The 'laying on of hands' is practised not only at the ordination of ministers and elders but also, where it seems appropriate, upon the sick.

Resources

Informal fellowship and sharing of Christian experiences will be encouraged. This might take place during or after a church service, in a home, or at a midweek meeting. Ministers and lay folk are encouraged to participate in training courses, either on a part-time basis or by correspondence.

An increasing number of people attend evangelical conventions and camps, the most popular being Keswick, Spring Harvest and Royal week, and find these spiritually helpful. The number attending the Annual Conference, held just after Easter, has increased over recent years. This in part is due to Bible exposition by a gifted speaker each morning.

Some will see disciplines such as fasting, tithing, intercessory prayer and meditation more than a loving duty, or obedience for obedience's sake: in the spirit of 'in giving we shall receive', they see such exercises as the avenue to spiritual nourishment.

Perhaps not fully appreciated, the spiritual growth that comes from suffering ought to be mentioned. The Countess herself experienced much suffering and bereavement, outliving her husband and most of her children. She would have understood and in hindsight have agreed with Romans 5:3-5.

Our missionary link

The missionary focus of the Connexion is on Sierra Leone, where there is an independent Connexion of churches. The Sierra Leone Mission currently supports ministers there, encourages theological and general training and provides resources for schools linked to the churches. Because of the recent unrest, we have been giving relief aid on a temporary basis.

The Fellowship of Churches of Christ

Spirituality is not a word that readily comes to mind in Churches of Christ. In our two major histories of the Movement there is hardly a mention of spirituality. Rather they have tended to emphasise theological positions and what is believed amongst the Churches, although there has been a variety of views on many matters of faith and order. The Churches were drawn together by a common understanding of the Church, based on New Testament teaching and witness and, in particular, the sacraments. The nature of the Church has been a major area of writing and exposition, as the Body of Christ, her essential unity in Christ, the objectivity of the Gospel and its ethical implications. Spirituality is closely related to theology and the practical outworking of that theology. However, in our 200 years of history, there have been certain commonly held features which have provided spiritual nourishment in our tradition:

The Sacraments

The vast majority of Churches have been unashamedly sacramentalist, avoiding both 'mechanical' and 'magical' interpretations, experiencing both Believers' Baptism and the Lord's Supper as channels of spiritual grace, engaging the will and reason as well as emotions. Dr William Robinson, for example, speaks of the 'real action' of the Lord's Supper as over against arguments about the 'real presence'.

Without exception, Communion or the Lord's Supper has always been the main act of worship each Sunday, blending the Service of the Synagogue (worship, praise, scripture and teaching, prayer) and the Service of the Upper Room. The insistence of the centrality of the Communion may have hindered the growth of Churches, being seen by those outside as a 'members only' event but the belief that first and foremost the Church is all about offering worship to God has predominated.

Believers' Baptism by immersion, for the forgiveness of sins, has been the norm through our history and remains for most a spiritual high point in their Christian pilgrimage, renewed regularly as they witness others making a similar commitment.

Where Church membership demands a high degree of personal commitment as well as an investment of considerable time in prayer and study, there is a corresponding high degree of spiritual satisfaction and reward. In the main, the Churches have been strongly anti-individualistic, believing in the corporateness of the Gospel. Individual piety and forms of mysticism have been foreign to their theology and experience.

In the last 25-30 years some congregations have ventured into family worship, or all-age worship.

Other factors

The leadership of ordained elders and deacons in most churches, often self-educated men, is given responsibilities for spiritual and sacramental ministry, which requires a high level of personal commitment. The congregation often draws their own spiritual strength from the example of such leaders. Weekly Bible study and prayer groups were very formative for generations and are becoming so again today in home groups, cell groups, Alpha and such courses.

The use of a common lectionary over many generations has been a strong unifying factor and a source of considerable spiritual strength. Churches generally took up and used the Joint Liturgical Group lectionary, but this is less the norm now as all-age material is available.

Churches of Christ (in the UK) have always been a small Movement and this has required a national and regional structure which supported a web of personal relationship. Partly for theological reasons but also as a geographical necessity, an intimacy between congregations has been developed and enjoyed, giving the scattered Movement a sense of their identity and a spiritual bonding and cohesion. Although universally 'congregational' in government, in the most part they have never been 'independents' in a strict sense, and always valued co-operation at national, regional and district levels. Such fellowship gatherings have been the source of many personal long friendships and spirituality significant.

Our Hymnody, and the few poets and hymn writers we have produced, reveal a deep personal spiritual understanding with undertones of the social implications of the Gospel, together with a call to personal holiness and saintliness. We are of course not alone in this. Various editions of the *Christian Hymnary* reveal how we have always been drawn on the rich ecumenical resources of worship material, suitably edited at times!

National magazines have always been very formative in influencing both our theology and personal spiritual practice over the years, often with an emphasis on what I would call a worldly spirituality. The absence of a magazine is a major weakness in the Churches' life today.

Conclusion

Over the years there seems to have been a corporate spirituality which has served to bind the Churches of Christ together. More recently as a result of the charismatic influences, spirituality has become a more dominant living issue at both an individual and corporate level and has begun to redress the intellectual position and plea of previous generations.

The Free Church of England

History

The Free Church of England is a much reduced body, today, compared to what it was at the beginning of the twentieth century. Although her roots go back to the Countess of Huntingdon's Connexion, our first recorded Minister is Revd James Shore who opened a Free Church of England place of worship in the West Country in 1844. The advance of the Tractarian Movement, in the 19th century, brought many more churches into existence and, in 1863, the Free Church of England was embodied in a Poll Deed duly registered in the High Court of Chancery. It was established as a separate branch of the church of God, with a Presbyterian ministry, a recognition of and provision for Episcopacy, and pledged to the Doctrines of the Church of England as set forth in the Thirty-nine Articles of Religion, and to the principles and practices associated with the Evangelical tenets of the Established Church. This position is still maintained today and the first article of the Constitution is of primary importance…. 'the Free Church of England declares its belief in the Holy Scriptures of the Old and New Testaments as the Word of God, and the sole rule of faith and practice.'

Worship

In recent years, the Denomination has been strengthened by Ministers and members from all the mainline denominations, including the Church of England. There are just twenty-six churches today, which reach as far as Exmouth in the south, to Workington virtually on the Scottish border. There is also scope for further expansion and new work as Christians of faith and conviction join us. Worship is varied but liturgical. But the Liturgy is not intended to cancel out extempore prayer and often, in a Service, both would be used. Strong emphasis is put upon pulpit ministry and expository Bible preaching would be a worthy aim.

Resources

Many churches have prayer meetings and Bible studies, Sunday School and youth work, and there is a new awareness of the need for evangelism and community service. Three new bishops have been recently consecrated, a new interest in the denomination and what it stands for is perceived, and expectancy is growing for the reversal of recent decline. Annual Convocation gives opportunity for discussion and counsel and Diocesan Synods allow opportunity for full lay participation.

Although we are not, as a Denomination, part of the Churches Together process, we pursue with increased interest all ecclesiastical development and long for the day when God's written Word will be the final criterion of all faith and practice. Our greatest desire is to see the Lord Jesus Christ accepted as Lord and Saviour and recognised as the sole Head of his Church. Those interested in our much-valued and deeply-loved Denomination can obtain more information from the Publications Steward, Free Church of England, 12 Elmfield Close, Exmouth EX8 3BJ. Tel: 01395 2271486.

The Old Baptist Union

The Old Baptist Union is a small group of evangelical Baptist churches dedicated to the proclamation of the Gospel. The Articles of Faith of the Old Baptist Union are organised after the scriptural principles of the General Baptists of 1611 and 1660. Known in the past as six principle Baptists, preaching and teaching the six foundation principles of Christ as found in Hebrews 6:1-2, we have a distinct set of articles of faith, and churches are governed according to a model constitution which allows for some local differences.

The Old Baptist Union is a close knit group of churches who are wholly evangelical, respect the autonomy of the local church, but are interrelated through a national executive which encourages, where it can, local vision and initiative.

Distinctive features

Firstly, an emphasis on the practice of the laying-on of hands after baptism for the receipt by faith of the fullness and gifts of the Holy Spirit. By this, we acknowledge no special powers in the person who lays on hands and prays for those who have been newly-baptised, simply it is a response in faith to a perceived practice of the early church. In order to live successful Christian lives, people need to be filled with the Holy Spirit. We pray in faith, expecting God to honour his promise to give the Holy Spirit to them that ask him. In practice as it is the experience of many people that baptism has become somewhat removed from an initial conversion, we now lay emphasis, not so much on receiving the Holy Spirit, but on being filled with the Holy Spirit and being equipped by the Holy Spirit for day-to-day life. It is the elders of the church who lay hands on the newly-baptised person.

Secondly, the Old Baptist Union has always maintained and practised the Church's ministry of healing. We encourage people to hear the words of James 5:14-15. Recognising that God heals in many and varied ways, we see that it is our privilege and responsibility to pray

for the sick, and especially for those who call for our help. Therefore
we have always practised this method of anointing with oil and prayer
of the elders as a means of involving the whole church in showing
concern for the healing of those who are ill.

Worship

In common with other Baptists, we would lay great emphasis on the
worship of the church and the preaching of the word as being
foundational to our understanding of church. All our churches are
closed membership, that is, only baptised believers may be members
of our churches, but all our churches celebrate an open communion
service, when all who love the Lord Jesus Christ as their Saviour may
share bread and wine with us. We also hold to the principle of the
church meeting being the place where the local expression of the body
of Christ will together find the will of God for their situation.

Individual Voices and Testimonies

*from within the Churches
sharing their own stories of spiritual nourishment*

Baptist

One of the primary areas in which I am sustained in my spiritual life and Christian Ministry is that of the gathered community of Believers in the local church, particularly through their faithfulness, their fellowship and their commitment to ministry and worship. The church also produces a prayer calendar each month, which I use daily. It includes a scripture reading, items for prayer and names of people from the church family to pray for.

Personally I am also sustained by my own spiritual discipline which involves an hour of contemplative silent prayer each morning and a 'check out' time each evening based on the Ignatian Examen. I have a silent retreat day each month in a local religious community. I see my Spiritual Director three or four times a year. Every other year I have an eight-day Individual Guided Retreat.

Another area of real sustenance and renewal is found in my relationship with others, both Christians from other traditions and non-Christians. There is a tremendous spiritual resource to be gained from the rich diversity of the Christian church as a whole, and in finding God outside the Christian community, indeed finding God in all things. Not least is this to be found in terms of what others expect to receive from and value in a Baptist Christian.

Hi, I'm Hannah. I will be ten years old in two months time. Here are some of the things which help me to be a Christian. Every week I go to Junior Sunday School. I enjoy going there because I meet my friends and I enjoy the games but I don't learn a great deal because I already know the stories.

The thing that helps me most is Spring Harvest because it is amazing to see people who are really dedicated to being Christians and it just makes me want to be like them. Every evening (or *most* evenings if I'm honest), I read Scripture Union *Snapshots* with my dad and I ask him questions. Last week we had a Holiday Bible Club at our church called *Space Race*. This helped me to realise that being a Christian is fun.

♫   I find music very encouraging – not just hymns, but a wide range including instrumental pieces as well as songs. With two small children, I don't often get time to sit and read the Bible as much as I would like, and what time I do have tends to be either very early morning or late at night when I am not really in the best state of mind for focussed reading. I find tapes of Scripture readings from Bible Society very useful as I can listen to the words and still be moving about. It's great to hear the Bible being read and it helps me keep up to date with my Bible studies as I can always go back and read through the parts I have heard when I get a minute.

Learning and education programmes are also helpful to me in my spiritual life. I think it's really important to relate my faith to my everyday life and I find it helps to have the point of view of other people when I'm thinking through or debating socio-political issues.

Black Pentecostal

The main elements of our worship are no different from other Christian churches; what is unique is our practice. As a people we are by nature expressive, enthusiastic and joyful, and this is reflected in our worship. We take the psalm literally: 'Make a joyful noise to the Lord... worship the Lord with gladness; come into his presence with singing. Enter his gates with thanksgiving, and his courts with praise.' (Psalm 100:1-2,4). Added to this, prayer, fasting, teaching and preaching of the Scriptures and the sharing of the testimonies of God's goodness are also emphasised during worship. The common Agape feast and sharing of meals are also essential elements. This is real 'Koinonia'.

The whole congregation is invited to participate, regardless of age or gender. This gives a great sense of identity, belonging and ownership. Talents and gifts are nurtured and allowed to develop, metanoia, faith in God's word and dependence on the Holy Spirit as enabler, empowerer, leader and director is paramount. Without the working of the Holy Spirit in our lives spontaneity is nought. We believe in the miraculous power of God through healing and deliverance and protection from the 'enemy'. Christianity for us is **a way of life**, with prayer as the simplest form of speech. In the words of James Montgomery's hymn:

Prayer is the soul's sincere desire,
uttered or unexpressed...

Prayer is the burden of a sigh,
the falling of a tear,
the upward glancing of an eye,
when none but God is near.

This is what moulds and shapes my character, allowing me to be 'open', adaptable, firm, yet enriched by other Christian traditions on our ecumenical journey, and deepens my faith in God, in such a way that words are inadequate to express it. Thanks and praise be to God.

ǫ 'All things work together for good for those that love God,' (Romans 8:28). I am learning more and more that in all situations, no matter how bad they may seem, God can and does bring good out of them if I trust his promise.

For example, over the Christmas period I had to be admitted to hospital. The hospital was 50 miles from home, so plans to spend the holiday with my family had to be cancelled. To make matters worse I did not feel unwell at all, in fact I felt better than I had done for a while. After a few days of self-pity, I started to get my thoughts round the fact that God could bring something good out of it all… and he did.

A lady, who I'd met through toddler group in my area, appeared on the ward one day and, when she saw me, came over to talk. She shared the news that her dad, who was on the same ward as myself, had just been informed that there was to be no more treatment for him.

She later left, but her mother and sister stayed for several days until he died. I was able to get alongside them, sometimes to talk, but on other occasions just sit with them. At the time I thought how weak I was, but I later learnt they were so glad that I was there, and able to support them.

He died on New Year's Eve, and I was able to mourn with them at his funeral.

The whole point of what I have written is that God keeps his promises to us. No matter how tragic, bad, tricky or inconvenient situations prove to be, I'm encouraged that God can and does bring good out of them if we trust him.

ǫ It is enough for me to know that in a confusing and ever changing world, God does not change. The goal-posts of life, such as work, relationships, finance, health and age, all move, but he is right where he was yesterday.

ℚ   What feeds me? What keeps me going in my Christian walk? In my head I was sure that I knew the answer - friends, family, church, special Bible passages and verses. All of which are important, but they are not what keep me going. To put into words my spiritual journey is very hard, and I have struggled to express my thoughts and feelings.

I have pondered the awesomeness of God, his love, his mercy, his grace, his boundless, ceaseless faithfulness to me; all of these do not even begin to touch on what I feel. Then I heard a song, and I knew that it spoke my heart; it spoke my life, it spoke the words that expressed why I continue on, following the Almighty God who gave His all for me.

The song *Alabaster Box* (based on Luke 7:37-38), written by Janice Sjostran, tells the story of a woman lost in sin, who despite the pain, and shame of what other people might think and say, approached Jesus. She knelt at his feet and poured out her love for him, by washing his feet with her tears, drying them with her hair and then breaking open the perfumed oil, which was the only thing in her life she felt was of any worth. Even though she could not forget her sinful life, she recognised that Jesus was the answer, the only way. So in coming to Jesus, she gave her all, her life, symbolised by the perfumed oil her only treasure. She gave back to him all the praise which was his due, for she recognised that she had been forgiven and that was why she loved him so much.

The song says:

'And I've come to pour my praise on him like oil, from Mary's Alabaster Box.
Don't be angry if I wash his feet with my tears, and dry them with my hair;
You weren't there, the night he found me;
You did not feel what I felt, when he wrapped his loving arms around me;
And you don't know the cost, of the oil, no; you don't know the cost,
of my praise; you don't know the cost, of the oil, in my Alabaster box'.

These words are true for me.   I will never be able to express how I felt the night Jesus came into my life and embraced me in his loving arms. Who am I? I am nothing, yet he loved me and died for me. What do I have? I have nothing but what he gives to bless my life.

What can I do? I can do nothing that he has not sanctioned and ordained. He is the air I breath, the beauty I see, and to give him less than all of me would be to cheat the one who is all to me.

My spiritual journey, and its nourishment, is life. For God is my life. To lose God is to lose life. He is the author and finisher of my faith. He keeps me going; my life is priceless to him, and therefore to not acknowledge him means to not acknowledge life.

❧   I find that being a Christian, although challenging, is very rewarding. One of my favourite Bible verses is 'I will bless the Lord at all times,' (Psalm 34: 1). Whether I am happy, sad, or feeling low, there is a Saviour I can turn to, who will bless me at all times, no matter what the situation is.

There have been times when I have been in great distress, and I had no one to turn to, but I have found that if you put your trust in the Lord (Proverbs 3:5-6), he will direct your path. He has taken me out of situations that no man or woman on earth could ever have taken me out of.

I like being a Christian because I have found joy in the Lord; the joy of the Lord is my strength. I don't have to worry about tomorrow, for the Lord looks after me, shelters me and protects me from all kinds of dangers. There have been times when I have wanted something, and even before I have prayed the Lord has provided it.

I serve a mighty God and that is my spiritual inspiration in being a Christian, and following the Lord Jesus Christ.

❧   In my life I have learned that there are three needs common to us all:

❖   The need to give to and receive love from family, friends or life partner.

❖ The need to have a sense of purpose and direction, a reason to be part of the world and to be alive.

❖ The need to have faith in oneself and in one greater than oneself, recognising one's personal talents, gifts, strengths and weaknesses come from God, and acknowledging that God, in whom there is no wrong, is able to correct our failures.

I have learned these values from my parents:

❖ The Bible teaches you to love others as much as you love yourself, not more than yourself!

❖ The importance of hard work, done to the best of your ability and done right!

❖ Don't think, you must know!

I have certain principles which I try to live by:

❖ Hate the things I do which are wrong, not the same wrong things I see in others, correct them, do them no more, and try to grow with God's help; but never hating myself.

❖ Be the first to say 'I'm sorry' firstly to God, then to anyone I have offended; try and take the higher ground, and never being a pushover.

❖ Try and live and walk God's way, with his help; try to stir up courage within myself to be positive about who I am.

❖ Admit that I'm not always right and concede gracefully when I'm wrong; accept instruction from older and from younger people, they sometimes know more than I do!

❖ Try to examine myself honestly and check myself against God's word; never believe I am bigger and better than I really am.

❖ Look after myself, physically, mentally, and emotionally, knowing that I am fearfully and wonderfully made in physique, stature and appearance. Accept that it is okay to say 'No,' where I'm not able to help, and the task is beyond my capabilities and talents, but try to help where I am able to.

❖ Continue to learn both academically and life's lessons, learning from my mistakes, learning from those who are older and wiser, but never scorning the wisdom of youth.

❖ Recognise that talents I have are God-given, I don't have rights over them.

❖ Acknowledge that my talents may be a struggle for others, whilst talents others have maybe a struggle for me – but that is okay.

❖ Never despise the fact I am not perfect, or don't have all the comforts I would like, for if I don't need it, I don't really have to have it. This will keep me trusting and depending on God.

Anglican

After I got over the shock of being asked the question 'what nourishes your spirituality?', a phrase floated into my mind, 'taste and see how good the Lord is' (Psalm 34:8). That led me on to think of the senses and how often they seem to be denied or left out of any thought of spirituality.

God has given me a world of sensations, which include music beautifully played in the open air and people like me listening to it with friends; a world of amazing sunsets over the Goodwin Sands; a world shot through with the glory of God, and the mess we men make of it; a world of walking the dog, while listening to Bach on a walkman, before the village wakes up.

As a sailor, I am still fed by the excitement of leaving the safety of port in a small boat, by the terror and exhilaration of the sea, and the wondrous sense of achievement of arriving safely in the next port.

I am fed by other people's stories of their journeys of faith, their courage and faithfulness, their trust in God, when all too often mine seems so shallow. I am fed by their simplicity in discovering that they don't always have to get everything right, their complexity in juggling impossible loads, relationships, work and family commitments.

My soul finds food in laughter, tears, meals shared, bread I've baked, wine I've made and shared with friends and strangers. My spirit soars in an unfamiliar church when I dare to ask someone to pray for two sick friends of mine, something I would never have done once upon a time.

I am nourished by the encouragement of others. This enables me to dance, play the trombone, act the fool and not mind what others think. I love to see others grow through being believed in, through discovering, as if for the first time, that they are truly loved and valued by God.

Occasionally I feel fed by worship, though not as often as I think the church might assume I will be. Producing radio programmes, writing and photography give me much food for thought but, perhaps interestingly, make me less satisfied with much worship.

A smile, a touch, laughter, the reality and risk of unconditional love, these all thrill me and feed me. Enjoyment of such food can be tempered by the scary thought of the provisional. Do I fill this moment, this meeting, this situation to the full? They won't return for a second shot. This is the moment, the time, the person.

℧   Spirituality according to my dictionary means things relating to the soul or spirit, or sacred things. I don't accord with the implicit dualism there, as some of my most spiritual moments have been rather physical, material (sensual) ones too. There have been rare occasions when they have occurred in church - Herbert Howells' *Collegium Regale Magnificat* and *Nunc Dimittis* frequently 'send' me. As ecclesiastical buildings go, the Halligrimskirkja in Reykjavik, Iceland, takes some beating, and Hereford Cathedral will always be a special place to me as the Blessing of our Marriage took place there.

Leaving the radio on in the middle of the night has provided me with two diverse musical experiences - one was *Awaken* by Yes, and the other Thomas Tallis's *Spem in Alium*. I've never achieved the same sense of peace again, no matter how many times I have heard those pieces.

There are also places - a bridge over the Kent motorway, the Tarn in Eltham, South East London, a view from the A4103 over Herefordshire in certain lights, assorted seascapes, the Byre Chapel of the Society of Our Lady of the Isles on Fetlar in Shetland, and St Peter-ad-Murum, Bradwell in Essex. Then there are waterfalls and any sort of sunset...

I have felt 'inspired' whilst writing, especially poetry, and sometimes whilst reading books: the light-dawning experience, when something clicks and you feel you have moved on in your understanding. This can be frightening, or frustrating. My development seems to be moving faster than and in a different direction from the average church service! The Certificate in Feminist Theology opened huge new vistas for exploration to me. The most shocking and exciting was discovering 'Female aspects of Deity' within the Judaeo-Christian tradition - the Shekhinah, the feminine Holy Spirit or Ruach, the Virgin Mary, numerous saints and holy women. This is where I have been stretched, angered, roused, exhilarated and quickened into new thinking and understanding - which I then can't express in the good old Church of England! I want to find new ways of expressing God which aren't exclusive, male and hierarchical, and to be able to use those words and actions without being made to feel subversive—though I'll carry right on being subversive if that's what it takes! Inevitably much of my growth has been inspired or guided by particular people - teachers, Girls' Brigade officers, college friends, many of whom were studying theology, colleagues, friends, even (on occasions!) clergy.

I also want to say that sex with someone I love very deeply and who loves me can be an intensely spiritual experience, as can the monthly grounding experience of bleeding and pain that I go through as a menstruating woman. This can be a creative time for me, or it can be awful! But it is in creativity that I probably feel most spiritual - making cakes or shortbread, potting up my beloved geraniums, writing poetry, taking photographs, stitching (cross-stitch is my most regular form of wordless prayer!), talking or writing letters to my friends, listening to or making music…

I've found something of a spiritual home in Taizé services, which I have led mainly because I could sing and was willing, but my experience is that they provide an oasis of calm in a busy world or office. There's a quietness and gentleness to the chants which I find soothing, and the silence (how rare silence is!) is as important as the song. Celtic Spirituality also appeals, as much as anything I suspect, because of its refusal to sideline daily mundane activity, and I strive to achieve this in my own life and work - with varying degrees of success.

Although my background is Catholic, I have been taught by Anglicans and Pentecostals and came to faith at the age of 11. It was when I came to university that God began to work greatly within me, gradually building up my faith step by step over much time and many years.

When I look back, there seem to be three main sources which build me up. One of these places is my time alone with God, especially when I am in situations of hardship and trial. Perhaps it is because they are the times when I seek him the most and realise that I cannot do things alone. During those times I need him undisputedly and completely, and it is then that his revelations hit me. He talks to me mainly through scripture and his Word and through the written words of Christian writers. It's then that I learn so much about myself and the person God intends me to be, and of his awesome power and his unfailing love and faithfulness. It's then, when I pray with all my heart, that I have my most precious times alone with Jesus – even though they are often my most difficult.

For the building up of my faith, fellowship with the church has been crucial – where I don't just mean the church as an institution, but the **people** who are the church. Although we sometimes fail, there have been times when God has taught me many important lessons through his people – through their actions or encouraging words or wise counsel and advice. Bible studies and prayer meetings, where I do not have to be afraid or defensive, have helped immensely, and having somebody – anybody – in the church whom I can trust and turn to has been crucial. When we have all come together, God has built me up through the preaching and teaching of his Word where I have been reminded of his truth and where I have been able to witness God in the lives of other people. Praise and prayer times have unlocked my heart where I have been encouraged to be genuine, allowing my past hurts to be healed and laying down heavy burdens, and letting myself be renewed.

God builds me up outside the church too—especially through my non-Christian friends. There are many challenging arguments that they put to me and although it can be hard and discouraging at times, God seems to use them to make me firm in my faith. Often they ask the most deep and challenging questions and I have to go over the foundations of my faith time and time again.

Nevertheless, God has been faithful and has watched over me – teaching me through his Word, comforting me in my prayer, strengthening me in my testing, and loving me through his people. Sometimes it has been painful and seems to take forever, but it is awesome to consider the work of God in us.

❧ My forty years on this earth has been like climbing up a mountain without appropriate equipment and clothing. I often ask myself 'why does everything have to be such hard work?' My faith in God, on a number of occasions, has almost been tested to the limit. My life is like an obstacle course and part of it is my own doing. Do I jump, go under, go forward, turn back or keep stumbling?

I have been a Christian over 25 years; my siblings, except for a brother and sister living in Jamaica, say 'no' to religion. My journey of faith has been slow and difficult, but I have been able to make it through because of Christian friends loving and supporting me through the good times and the bad times. By the grace of God, with support from the church, family, friends, I manage to negotiate most of the obstacles without turning back. My faith is priceless and I will fight to keep hold of it, and to share my journey of faith knowing that Jesus Christ lives within me, loving me, giving guidance, providing a beacon, security, answering my prayers, and giving me unlimited access to my Creator.

I try to lead one life through church, work and home: to do otherwise would be making a mockery out of my belief in God and a poor witness to those I come into contact with.

My journey of faith took a severe blow two and a half years ago. Without warning, I was thrown into a horrific nightmare. Up until then my life had been fairly smooth. I thoroughly enjoyed my work as a social worker, and I was due to start a course that would have enhanced my career and my work in my church. Then my good health was suddenly taken away from me whilst on holiday abroad. I needed major surgery, and I was in horrendous pain. My head was packed full of negative thoughts, 'I am not going to go home, I am going to die, I'm so alone, and thousands of miles from home'. I had to shake myself, which was very difficult, and call upon the one person who could help me through the nightmare – Jesus Christ. From that moment I felt safe in the knowledge I was no longer alone in my confusion and pain.

As I lay in that hospital bed overlooking the Indian Ocean, I could see the fishermen casting their nets. The scene reminded me of the fishermen in Galilee who were to be Jesus' disciples, and their obedience in leaving their nets without looking back.

Very shortly after my admission to hospital things took a dramatic turn for the better and I could begin to see light shining through the darkness. The parish priest came to visit me just before my operation. He was an angel sent to give me comfort. Waking up after surgery, I found strangers in my room praying. They were from the local Anglican church and they had been keeping a vigil through intercessory prayer. They were not strangers, but sisters through the blood of Jesus Christ. It was like waking up and finding a priceless gem.

The main sources of my nourishment are the Word of God, and praying friends. On many occasions prayers have been answered, but not in the way I was expecting. God speaks to me directly or confirmation comes from friends. Whenever I visited a client for the first time I would send up an arrow prayer for support, for I did not know what was behind the door and prayer was my armour to protect me from the unknown. If I had any doubts about the power of my Creator, they have now been banished forever. My God is real, he is alive and provides everything that is good in unlimited quantities.

Members of Countess of Huntingdon's Connexion

   I believe that spiritual nourishment must be obtained from a mixture of sources. For me, the three that provide the basis for a healthy, spiritual diet are Bible study, prayer and fellowship. If we are to know more about God and the way in which He wants us to live our life, it is vital that we study his Word. The Bible gives us a clear and specific guide to what is acceptable in God's sight. Prayer is our personal communication with God through the Lord Jesus. It provides us with the means to praise and worship our Creator on a personal level. It also enables us to request his help and guidance, which can give us confidence and reassurance that he has every situation under his control.

It is important for Christians today to remember that although they are in this world they are not of it. After spending the majority of the week in a non-Christian working place, the fellowship of other Christians on a Sunday or perhaps at a weekly Bible study, can help us re-focus on the Lord and what he wants and expects from us. It is also an opportunity to share problems and experiences with like-minded people who will support and pray for each other. Without fellowship, it can be easy to copy and follow the lifestyle of non-believers.

Although I appreciate that these are just a few ways in which a Christian can receive spiritual nourishment, I have found personally that when I have got these three in operation, the others seem to follow.

   This is the personal view of a Christian who happens to be a member of the Countess of Huntingdon's Connexion, which is a very small denomination comprising a group of virtually autonomous evangelical Churches. My background prior to becoming a member of this Connexion is of evangelical Anglican and Methodist fellowships. Therefore I feel my view of the subject is formed more by my own Christian journey than by any affiliation to a specific denomination. Conversely, I can see some strands of my argument unravelling as I go on to discuss those views!

When we are seeking a new fellowship after moving to live in a new area, I think we are seeking the things which will meet our individual spiritual needs. I believe it is a wholeness that we seek, a Christian superstore that provides all we personally require. I would not presume to suggest such an institution could exist, as churches are all made up of imperfect human beings (particularly me!), but the argument still holds that we seek the church that best meets our needs.

The Christian's life is a journey, and a journey not without its difficulties. The Bible tells us to expect trials, hardships and all-out persecution, and to share one another's sadness and joy, to bear one another's burdens and to care for each other. To be part of a fellowship which does share joy and grief, centred on Christ, is for me the essential backdrop against which Christians living in this world can receive (and hopefully give) spiritual nourishment. I would not treat lightly the obvious and critical ingredients of nourishment which must include regular Bible study, prayer, communion, worship, and hearing the Word of God expounded. However, I firmly believe that these elements must be put alongside sacrificial giving of time, talents, and other resources, and be anchored within a loving fellowship.

In summary, I believe that holistic biblical Christianity, lived out as part of a fellowship which is trying to be Christ's salt and light in the twenty-first century, and showing the relevance of Christ to the society of which we are a part, will be truly nourished by the Spirit both corporately and individually. Only by taking on board the whole of the Christian lifestyle can we expect to receive a fully balanced nutrition.

    My working life is both challenging and rewarding, exhausting and invigorating, sad and happy. To meet the challenges of each day, I cannot leave the house without an adequate breakfast. In fact, if I didn't have it, by mid-morning I would not be coping well. Just as my body needs nourishment from food, so my spirit needs God's nourishment. However it is not, like the food we eat, hit and miss, taken as needed, good for me or bad for me. God's nourishment is purely for my good. It is constant, it is present in so many ways, it is a living thing, and I cannot live without it. Spiritual nourishment comes through God's presence with me, in all things, through all things, seen and unseen.

A fountain pen uses up ink, writing and leaking, and it needs to be refilled to work again. I am like that. I am constantly used up. Age is now no longer on my side, I am prone to depression and self-doubt, but talking to God, hearing him, seeing him, singing about him, reading of him, provides the spiritual nourishment to fill me again.

As teenagers, in our church, we share in the main forms of spiritual nourishment that our denomination as a whole does. These include reading the Bible, listening to sermons, being involved in Sunday School, praying, and joining with other Christians at events such as at our Connexional Youth Conference or concerts by contemporary worship leaders like Noel Richards and Dave Bilborough.

To us young people, however, it is the social aspects of spirituality that are the most important. It is important to us to feel that we belong, that we are part of a family or group of friends. This is why, to us, the chat before and after a service is just as important as the service itself. Sharing how we feel with others over a coke and tube of Pringles can have just as much impact as a good sermon. Because of this we are involved in activities such as the Soul Survivor Youth camp and have set up a youth cell where we can encourage each other in our Christian lives.

Methodist

As a youngster I received sound teaching in a Methodist Church Sunday School. As a young person I would have considered myself to be a 'plodder' in the faith, always involved and endeavouring to deepen my understanding. Throughout my professional life I have helped young people and encouraged their worship and fellowship groups.

My own Christian life has been nourished over the years by regular attendance at the annual Keswick Convention, and this was particularly important since my work took me to different places and so I did not establish roots in any one church. The Bible studies and seminars at the Keswick Convention have been led over the years by ecumenical scholars and evangelists, and the experience is always inspiring and encouraging.

Only recently, however, has my faith and understanding taken a leap forward and been challenged. I was invited to participate in the Disciple course as a student and as a leader. Not only has it been an immense privilege to share alongside fellow Christians, but my own faith has been challenged and rewarded. I now look forward to another year of 'Disciple' and would encourage all Christians of whatever denomination to join such a course and to grow spiritually.

Recently, a lady unexpectedly blessed me, as I waited for change in her shop. She may have blessed everyone who entered and bought from her, but my spirits lifted and I carried on my shopping in a cheerful manner. A little later, another lady told me that she had prayed for good weather for the village Gala celebrations. This lady has never shared such an intimate detail before and again my spirits rose. Twice in one day, unexpectedly and not from Christian friends, God broke through and showed me that his presence is everywhere.

Within the church we have a tendency to believe that unless we are busy and seen to be doing religious things and supporting Christian ventures, God is not at work in this world. I am continually surprised and much relieved by moments such as I have described. God is not restricted to ancient stone walls and spires, but is alive within the hearts and minds of his people, who take him with them as they move from the Sunday service or the weekly fellowship into the world at large.

My Christian home is within the Methodist Church in the Peak District, a scattering of small chapels with small, devoted, yet vulnerable congregations. Since the 'seventies, much ecumenical work has been done to bring together the Christian denominations for worship. The Parish Church, with its history seeping out of its columns and gargoyles, fills me with a sense of mystery and continuity. The community of saints who have worshipped there, despite the political and religious upheavals that dot our history, reminds me of the faithfulness that I am called to share and continue in this place. The church releases peace and hope and stability in a world crazed by the desire for change.

With roots in the Scottish Presbyterian Church, a time in the Baptist Church, then marriage into the Methodist Church, my experience has given me an independence to seek out ways of fulfilling the need to understand Jesus and finding ways to bring him alive. I have recently been introduced to the work of Philip Yancy, an American writer, who takes a refreshing look at Jesus, in *The Jesus I Never Knew*. He challenges the images and stories of Jesus, and encourages a closer, more honest, look at the Son of God, who has the capacity to change the individual. People don't find it easy to talk about Jesus as if He is a magnificently wrapped present that is too beautiful to open. When there is courage to mention his name in a spirit of knowing him, then there is nourishment.

Music is becoming a more important ingredient in worship for me. It can be loud, exhilarating gospel music, step-pounding Jewish rhythms, or quiet meditative worship songs. All can increase my desire to worship and feed my spirit. The singing and music-making of the Methodist Church encourage this, as does membership of the large ecumenical Sheffield Celebration Choir. Through weekly practice and worship, through concerts and leading worship in churches, concert halls, and in the open air, God nourishes us through music and words and togetherness, regardless of denominational differences.

The discovery that faith is inspired and ignited in an abundance of ways, generates the exhilarating thought that God is not bound by buildings, ideas, expressions but is creative and visionary in the methods He uses to reveal himself.

A number of things nourish me in my faith, and until asked to write this piece I didn't realise how complex an issue this is. Primarily, my nourishment arises out of my own personal need. Any particular aspect would have no nourishing effect if I did not go to 'the table' hungry. As within Methodism there is ample opportunity for lay ministry, I find I am called to serve in a number of different ways, and in doing so I am conscious of my lack of resources. In seeking personal help I find my faith is nourished in the process because I see God supplying my need either through others or directly.

As a lay preacher leading worship, I am conscious of the need of the congregation and my responsibility to provide the opportunity for those people to meet with God and worship him. When I see God working through me, or in spite of me, my faith is confirmed and strengthened. As I work at trying to understand the scriptures with a view to sharing them with others, I find their truths and significance become more clear and relevant to me. As a result I become excited by the Word of God and my faith is nourished.

I find that praying for people in need makes me hungry for a deeper and more effective prayer life. This, I hope, steers me away from the superficial, as I engage in the variety of prayer forms used within Methodism, including liturgical, extempore, meditative, and silent prayer. I find all of them particularly beneficial at different times, but I am most challenged and stretched and as a result nourished through personal intercessory prayer.

As a Christian of some years I feel I should know more than I do, but I find difficulty in finding the time and concentration for serious reading. However, I am often inspired by the clarity with which some people are able to address, if not explain, aspects of theology and practical Christian living. I find my spirituality is enabled to develop by having a sound background of Christian teaching, so although not a great nourishment in itself, reading provides the background that enables me to receive nourishment in other ways.

Holy Communion, I now realise, is probably what nourishes my faith on the most personal level. Whatever the form of service, I find receiving the elements deeply moving and sustaining.

So there is no one activity to which I could turn to nourish my faith or recommend others to adopt to build themselves up spiritually. Whilst we should all rejoice that 'our cup runneth over' there is a very real sense that we need to involve ourselves in sacrificial worship and service so that we can continue to receive what God gives in abundance.

⚖ For over thirty years I have been blessed by being a member of a church which has cared about nurturing the spiritual life of its members. Looking back and reflecting over those many years, the words which come to mind are pause, prayer and participation.

Back in the 'seventies when the retreat movement in Methodism was in its infancy, I would join about thirty members of the congregation on an annual silent retreat. I was encouraged to explore other retreats around the country offered by retreat houses of different denominations. In more recent times Quiet Days and Quiet Afternoons have become a regular church activity. Church family weekends and Awaydays, far removed from our usual city centre location, provide opportunities to pray and play, to spend time together in fellowship in a rural setting, which nurture mind, body and spirit. These times to pause offer us space as individuals, all leading frantic and stressful lives, nourishment as community, enjoying each other's company, sharing our journeys and finding time in those pauses to connect with each other and with God.

When our church premises were refurbished, a Quiet Room was made available for prayer and silence. A small group of us meet regularly to pray together, with words and silence, and others find it an oasis to sit and be still for a short break in the busy city centre. Sunday evening services are sometimes reflective using meditations, chants, writings from the spiritual classics, poetry and music to encourage us to go beyond the prayer of words, exploring the difference between thinking about God and experiencing God in our everyday lives. These services are an important influence in making connections between the example of Christ's life in the Gospels and how it connects with my own daily activities, discovering something about the essential nature of my humanity and the humanity of God in Christ as shown in the Gospels.

Participation in the social outreach of a city centre church follows quite naturally from the time set aside to be quiet with God, and from the concerns shared in prayer for life in the city streets around us. The time to pause in silence and in prayer ensures that it is not possible to settle for a comfortable religion. With homeless people sleeping rough in the church porch, and social work activities updated in the weekly church notices, we are continually confronted with our collective responsibility for the injustice, pain and suffering confronting us in the world in which we live. Belonging to a believing community, I am offered opportunities to live out my spirituality in service alongside others.

I thank God for a church which points the way to silent pauses and the exploration of my relationship with God through prayer, not as an egotistical ivory tower experience, but in the creative participation of building God's kingdom through community and fellowship, social action and concern.

Quaker

I came to the Religious Society of Friends after spending more than fifteen years in a spiritual wilderness. I had been brought up as an Anglican, but began to drift away from the church in my late teens after encountering a form of extreme evangelical fundamentalism which starved my spirit and destroyed my faith. My desert years were not satisfying to me: I knew something was missing from my life, and my mid-life religious quest began.

Although I had attended some Quaker meetings in my twenties, my first visit to Sutton Meeting in April 1982 was a transforming experience. As soon as I sat down the silence enfolded me and I knew the Presence. I knew both that I had come home and that I was setting out. These two aspects of that memorable morning have never left me. Perpetually renewed in Meeting is the sense of the deep silence of the mysterious God who is beyond what my mind can grasp, yet from whom new images arise, to stretch, challenge, heal and transform me. Of course not all meetings for worship reach the deep silence, and certainly not for all of the time. Worshipping in this way is often difficult and is vulnerable to many kinds of distractions and interruptions, but it 'works' enough of the time to continue to nurture and sustain me.

Increasingly I find I do need other sources of nurture. The insights of the mystics have opened my heart and mind to new ways of approaching God. The writings of Julian of Norwich enabled me to discover new, liberating, images of God as comforter, sustainer and healer, existing as the very ground of my being. More recently I have become increasingly drawn to the *via negativa* and to practising the prayer of silence which, I have found, helps to keep me more centred, more aware of the Spirit in my daily life.

Using images is an important part of my spiritual journey. My teaching ministry has been focussed on combining head and heart learning and using the arts in a 'kindergarten simple' personally expressive way, in order to release the action of the Holy Spirit in people's lives. I have many of my own paintings, collages, weavings and writings which are vivid testimonies to the truth that this process has worked powerfully in my own life too. Other people's images also feed my soul and I find them especially in poetry, novels, paintings and other visual arts, and music.

Other sources of nurture come from people, from fellow Quakers and others who have given encouragement, love and support. There are two people who are of special importance. One of these, relatively recently arrived in my life, is a Benedictine nun whom I visit for spiritual direction. I have been able to pour out my problems, discoveries, anguish and joy, and have been truly and completely heard by someone able to discern what lies beneath, and where God is at work. The whole experience has been, and continues to be, one of growth and adventure. The other person has been in my life for much longer. I am blessed to have a partner who is on a similar spiritual journey, without whom my steps would have been slower and more faltering. To receive love, support and discernment from the person who walks beside you, is indeed a pearl of great price.

⅋ I was born and brought up as a Roman Catholic, and was going to become a priest. However, I had - and still have - trouble with the idea of faith. There are things I believe, and people I trust, but fundamentally I need to *know*. This is still the basis of my spiritual life. The Roman Church gave me a basic religious upbringing, a love of art, music and chanting, and many things to question.

After leaving, I searched, and eventually attended a lecture by a Buddhist monk on the *Kalama Sutta,* where the Buddha advises seekers to only accept teachings that are helpful, and not just because they are in a holy book, or taught by priests, teachers or tradition. This was what I needed. I became a Buddhist, and learned to meditate. This *Sutta* is still fundamental to my spiritual life.

I also explored Spiritual Healing, because one of my friends had a miraculous cure through prayer. For several years I carried out research, witnessed many 'miracles', and discovered that prayer really works. However, I also found that effective prayer is not limited to any one religion or practice. This led me to an understanding that God is real, not the God of religion, but one that is beyond all our concepts and limitations.

I first came to the Quakers because I thought their silent meeting was a meditation group. Quakers believe in 'that of God' within each person. We meet in silence, not for meditation of a personal kind, but to realize the presence of God and allow God to speak to us. Spiritual healing was an essential part of the ministry of early Friends, as it was of the ministry of Jesus. In spite of this, and of the work of The Friends' Fellowship of Healing, I am saddened to say that many contemporary Friends will not accept it as a part of Quaker life.

Religion for me must be practical, and bring results here and now. Peace, non-violence and a compassionate restlessness towards the suffering of the world are essential. Quaker Christianity and Buddhism share these. My respect for the Christian basis of Friends enabled me to apply for and be accepted into membership. I made no secret of my Buddhism. I hold that the life and teachings of Jesus are 'an inspiration to try to live up to for my next ten lifetimes'. I now see myself as both a Quaker and a Buddhist, (not, however, a 'Quaker-Buddhist'' or a 'Buddhist-Quaker').

I do not find conflict between my Buddhism and Christianity. Those who look for conflict can find it, but only in doctrine, and not in the mystical aspects. It is language which causes division. The Pure Land tradition of Buddhism which I practise emphasises the Inward Light and the Great Compassion, which it calls 'Amitabha'; George Fox called this same Light 'Christ Jesus', and knew God as Love. Language will always differ, but the essence is One. My daily practice is meditation on this Light, invoking the Holy Name (which has many forms) and healing prayer for those who ask me for help.

I have a vision of the Buddha and Jesus meeting, embracing, sharing the deepest silence, laughing, crying, exchanging stories and healing those who come to them for help. They never mention religion, and certainly do not debate the relative merits of Nirvana or the Kingdom of Heaven. It is such a vision that feeds my spiritual life.

I would have no spirituality to nurture if on another of my attempts to escape God's grip on me, I had not been persuaded to try an Ignatian retreat. The retreat had three very important outcomes. First, it showed me how to use the Bible with imagination and thus freed me from guilt at the mind-numbing effect traditional Protestant Bible study had on me; and it led me to

Friendly Bible study, a rich source of illumination and guidance.

Second, I took the advice to do a 'Myers-Briggs Type Indicator', which showed me what were likely to be the most nurturing spiritual practices for me - and thus I came to the Religious Society of Friends. Third, it gave me the first of three wonderful women with whom I have shared a 'Spiritual Friendship' over the years.

Meeting for morning worship with the other members of the ecumenical 'Community of Households', in which I live, roots me in the reality of other people's spirituality. The tradition that feeds this, and gives me the gift of this reality, is in the Psalms, not only for us at 'The Neighbours Community' but for all those other communities for whom the Psalms are the core of their prayer. The saying of a psalm each day makes me feel supported and in some way united with all those other people who, from the beginning, have expressed how it is for them before God in this way.

Daily chores, cooking and particularly weaving and spinning, 'the work of my hands', ideally requiring my complete attention, drive away the demons of anxiety and worry, allowing me to be 'open to the Light, from whatever source it may come'. Becoming aware that I need to see sometimes routine tasks, as well as the times when I am weaving a rug or spinning some special yarn, as times of mindfulness and life enhancement, has made me less resentful of the time spent on necessary maintenance.

I am nurtured and energised when I make the connection between the 'Now' experience of the Spirit in Meeting for Worship and my understanding, through reading and study, of the tradition in which I stand - and most particularly when I stand in some often crumbling and isolated church in Greece or Turkey and feel I can stretch out and almost touch the past. I feel my feet are where someone stood who knew Jesus, perhaps heard the apostles, or met St Paul.

Similarly energising is the contrast between our often austere Meeting Houses and the sense-tingling frescoes, icons, candles and incense: the stillness of a Quaker Meeting for Worship and the movement, bowing, crossing, kissing and clasping of Orthodox and Catholic worship - and particularly the (for me) throat-catching moment in the worship of the Turvey communities when they open their arms, palms up, and say 'Our Father'.

All these things are good for me, and most of them come to me in the normal round of my life. Then there are the Glory moments which can be planned for, such as visits to art galleries and exhibitions, concerts and concentrated listening to music, or going to the ballet. My spirituality would be poorer without them, and I need to make space for them, too.

    I am asked how I look after my spiritual life.

What can I share? I am aware of being nurtured, but how has this been experienced?

It has seemed to be a Word spoken to me throughout my life. I heard it on a cold clear Northern winter night when I was five. I looked at the familiar sky with its myriads of stars and was filled with awe, with a sense of deep relationship. Later I heard it in wide-open spaces, secret silent places, murmurings of trees and streams, the constant surge of the sea. In loving and enjoying these things I am still sometimes grasped by that deeper grace of awareness—as I might now express it—of God in all things; all is sacramental and nurtures my spirit.

My one contribution to this seems to be a willingness to be open to its possibility. But since I am by nature a solitary person I have had to work hard at extending this openness. It has been difficult to risk sharing my most treasured or most painful experiences. But it has been—is—necessary, for numinous awe was followed by a developing awareness of a God who speaks in me an intensely personal Word, a Word of powerful and incarnate Love. The Spirit of Christ calls into communion, community and ministry. I am still discovering the joy and pain of what that means in human relationships and I still agonise over 'things ill done' which once I 'took for exercise of virtue'. I am helped by the Quaker advice to 'take heed to the promptings of love and truth' in my heart and to 'trust them as the leadings of God...'.

And the Word speaks to me in and through others, not only with support, sharing, encouragement and affection, but also in rebuke or even in unkindness. The Spirit guides in all of these if I will listen, reflect and wrestle. In this I am strengthened by Quaker meetings for worship, shared learning and healing prayer, and by a small ecumenical contemplative (Julian) prayer group.

Guidance and growth have come through Christian and Interfaith retreats and courses and through spiritual writings from faiths other than mine, especially among these the Buddhist guidance of Thich Nhat Hanh –'beautiful flowers in other gardens'. And so I have learned more of the ministry of being present - present in the present moment, present with others, present for others: the blessedness, for an over-conscientious soul, of 'sitting at the feet...'. From yesterday's essential language of study, much reading, much reflection and a structured prayer life, I have been brought to a seemingly unstructured inward contemplative life, an ocean depth on which the waves of outward busyness are carried.

This life is nurtured by the inner remembrance of God's love. I say 'remembrance' advisedly for the consolation of awareness is sometimes long withheld. In the desert, in trust, I learn that my roots need to go still deeper. My faith has gone through long periods of 'what if?'. I have questioned and abandoned much. But the eternal Word is still being spoken as I wait in the Light which 'searches me and knows me' and in the Love which has enfolded me in my life's greatest sorrows as in its greatest joys. It has yet to reveal tomorrow's voice.

––––––––––––

℞ I was born into a Quaker family where I was lovingly nurtured throughout my childhood. My spiritual roots are firmly within the Christian Quaker tradition which I accepted unquestioningly; the life and teaching of Jesus and the radical ministry of George Fox have given me a pattern for living. My spiritual journey has never deviated from this primary route, I have never felt the need. As a child and a young adult I was influenced by the faith and example of older, experienced Friends in whom the grace of God was apparent. Not only they, but those of other traditions, transformed my thinking; for example a Scottish Baptist minister who gave inspiring sermons and nurtured me through his love and friendship.

There is no doubt that belonging to a Quaker community, both locally and nationally, is my most important source of spiritual nurture. Our Meetings for Worship, our worship sharing and study groups, our Testimonies, social concerns and activities, are the spiritual wellspring which affirms my faith. A shared faith community provides fellowship and support, it is a service and a gift we give to each other. In times of sadness or tragedy, as well as joy, we are bound more closely together. Being human and fallible we also have to cope with our disunity and inadequacies, sometimes a painful but necessary learning experience.

The most difficult and testing time for me is isolation or absence from this community. Being clear about my priorities and finding a regular time for reflection or devotion on my own are difficult disciplines where I frequently fail. I know that spiritual nurture and growth are hindered when I am over-burdened with the complexities of life. Joining a healing group recently has been helpful. The practice of inner visualisation and holding someone or a situation in the Light helps to focus my attention, and is a form of prayer. On occasions when I am feeling distracted or exhausted, sitting still for as short a time as five minutes and regaining an inner calm has proved remarkably beneficial.

Another source of spiritual nurture is almost any form of creativity. I started painting flowers in my off-duty during nursing training and have found since that 'losing myself' in creative activity is often not only therapeutic, it lifts my spirit. In nature there is always solace and peace for the soul, as there is in many forms of human creative achievement, in art, architecture, music and words. Solitude is necessary and good at times but I should not do well on my own for long. To share an experience with an individual or a group to whom I feel spiritually close, is a form of communion. At its most profound it goes beyond an emotional response, this is when I meet that other person or people in the things which are eternal; at these moments I feel that I am in the presence of God, encompassed and nurtured.

———————————————————

Roman Catholic

I would consider myself an ecumenical, Catholic Christian. My fundamental roots are within the Catholic Church but from an early age I was encouraged to explore and find the riches of other Christian Churches. I attended Mass in the Catholic Church with my father, Sunday School in our local Methodist Church with friends, and ended the day with Evensong in the Anglican Church with my mother. This liberal cosmopolitan worship has persisted throughout my life. I find myself nurtured and nourished in a whole variety of traditions. My life with God has been important since early childhood; God has always felt very real and I move easily between churches knowing deep within that the God we all worship is one and the same.

A common thread of nourishment throughout my life has been a love of Scripture, begun in the sharing of Bible stories with my mother. At Teacher Training College, at the time of the Second Vatican Council, the Scriptures came alive for me and I was excited and enthused as I saw the depth and wealth of meaning through my studies. This love has deepened through the years, particularly since a week of Accompanied Prayer when through praying the Scriptures I began to feel and express the intimacy of relationship the Creator has with each creature, fully experienced in the life of Christ and my commitment with Christ to the furthering of the reign of God.

People too have nourished me and brought me ever closer to knowing the God who loves me. People I have known personally throughout my life have kept alive the belief that my individual relationship with God was important and my inner truth was to be valued always. People like Nelson Mandela, Martin Luther King and Teilhard de Chardin whose lives have inspired me, as do the words of Micah 'to act justly, to love tenderly, to walk humbly with my God.' Words and phrases that have been spoken to me have sent me further along the path of discovering and recognising more and more of the me God created, and the purpose of my life. The life-changing moment during bereavement counselling following my mother's death when I was asked 'What do you want?' and I took it seriously for the first time ever, is one of many I can own.

Liturgy and music too have nourished my spirit, from the mystery of the Latin Mass, the great ceremonies of the Church's year through family celebrations of life and death to the more intimate and gentle acts of worship in retreats and weeks of accompanied prayer, together with the worship of Iona and Taizé. Celebrations with children and school assemblies have often been points of growth for me, never mind the children I was teaching.

Times of silence, my daily Examen (the practice of reviewing the day before God as part of one's night-time prayer), and retreats are the everyday vital and essential nourishment. The meeting with God in the very depths of my being enables me to reach out and do all that I do with a new consciousness and meaning.

---

၅၃   A great deal of my understanding of being a Catholic stems from the strong commitment from those who educated me—my parents and Catholic teachers—who to some extent formed my character and therefore the person I am. They were all in harmony in believing what it really meant to be a Catholic, that the gift of the Catholic Faith was the greatest and most precious of all the gifts that I was ever to receive from any source whatsoever. Nothing that I would ever be given could ever surpass it.

In having this gift I was taught to pray; that is to talk to God as a friend having complete confidence that He loves me and I am special to him. I can take my joys as well as my sorrows to him. He will understand all, listen and give help and reply to all I ask, not always in the way I expect, but answers and help come in his time.

The gift of the Mass, and the Sacraments mean a great deal to me. In Baptism we are claimed by God for himself. As we get older we are enriched by the Sacraments of forgiveness, renewal, comfort, and most especially himself in the Holy Eucharist. All these gifts surround us with love and it therefore follows that we should be willing and wanting to pass on the love to one another in whatever way we can, both spiritual and temporal, when we see each other in need.

The Church gives us guidelines on how this should be done, encouraging us in charity to others, distinguishing right from wrong, using our discernment and conscience and sometimes courage in making and standing by principles and beliefs. It teaches us to react to others with understanding and tolerance even when this can be most difficult and strain all our resources. The two great commandments are firstly to love God, and secondly to love our neighbour as ourselves. If we use these two tenets there can be no greater enrichment in our lives and we will always have peace within ourselves when we practise them to the best of our ability.

I must always remember that my actions will be seen as Catholic - this carries a responsibility on my part to my Catholic faith. It is not always distinguished by others what the Catholic teaching and feeling really is, compared to what is actually practised at times. We all stumble at times and at those times we must have an absolute confidence in immediate forgiveness—even before it is asked. Can anything be more enriching?

I know that my Catholic faith has enriched my life, as having that faith has made me the person that I am or hope to be in the future. Whether I have made the most of this gift, or even become a small fraction of what I should be, remains to be seen. I am certain that without my Catholic faith I would not recognise the person I have become, and I would most certainly be in some ways different.

   My childhood years were nourished by my mother's strong Catholic faith, which she passed on to me, and by the nuns at my little convent school, which I loved. In my early teenage years my Catholic faith was sorely tested when my mother became a Quaker and encouraged me to follow her, but the roots were already in deep for me. I chose to go to a Catholic College of Education where I made some lovely Catholic friends who nourished my faith, and we attended daily Mass together.

My Catholic faith was tested once more when I moved down to North London from Yorkshire and was feeling somewhat homesick. I attended the Catholic church but hadn't found it easy to make friends there. Someone recommended the local Baptist church as being very friendly, so I started going there for a few weeks and was almost overwhelmed by friendliness. But I felt guilty about my Catholic roots and one day returned home from work to find a visiting card had been left by the local priest. Through him I discovered a whole new side to the Catholic church through a small charismatic prayer group he took me to, and I soon made some Catholic friends locally.

This time, when I moved, I had no trouble making friends through the local Catholic church. I discovered a charismatic prayer group straightaway which nourished my faith, and joined a group of young people from the church with whom to attend social events such as bowling and rambling. Best of all I met my husband, who was very strong in his faith and with a strict upbringing by Jesuit priests at his school in Italy. My husband finds encouragement in these words, 'each believer is thus a link in the great chain of believers. I cannot believe without being carried by the faith of others, and by my faith I support others in the faith'. (*Catechism of the Catholic Church,* English translation published by Geoffrey Chapman, London 1994. Article 2.)

My faith is nourished by my involvement in the parish, by the people I meet at church, by regular Mass attendance and receiving Holy Communion. It has been further nourished by seeing my children grow up, receive the sacraments, serve on the altar and play in the folk group. I have a lovely group of friends with a great faith who have taught me a lot, and we regularly pray together.

I have met some wonderful priests who have encouraged and nourished my faith; I have also had some experiences with priests which have tested my faith. But there has always been someone stronger in their faith who has come into my life at the critical times and made sure I didn't lose mine. I'm sure someone up above has been watching over me. Thanks be to God.

Since being asked to write down my thoughts on this subject, I have thought hard and long, and could put down many learned sentences taken from passages written by great Catholics. But for me, none of these need necessarily be true.

By an 'accident of birth' I was born into a Christian environment, whereas by a similar 'accident' my neighbour was born into a Muslim environment. We have differing faiths, but both require the same degree of nurturing. In past centuries, both faiths have perhaps misguidedly taught their followers that there can be only one true faith.

I do not consciously know what maintains and nourishes my faith. I do know what assails it. Often I think hard about all the arguments as to why there is no God, and probably more relevent to my Catholic faith and teaching, why Jesus Christ was a great man of his time, but not the Son of God. I think to myself in this modern day and age where nothing happens that is not almost immediately common knowledge 'what if Christ came to this earth again, who would believe that he was indeed the Son of God?' Imagine the miracles he would have to perform to convince the doubting masses - myself included. In a world assailed by so many natural disasters both large and small, it would be all very easy to believe that it is all just a part of the natural evolution of the universe governed only, as many eminent scientists say, by the natural laws of physics. I suppose that the fact that these eminent men can agree that there are laws which govern the behaviour of the universe helps me to believe that this behaviour is not just random chance but has been put in place by some overall power which we know as God.

The next part is more difficult. Is Christ the Son of God? I was born into a Christian environment so all my early teaching was based on that very premise. For me, Jesus is the Son of God, and what he has promised to his followers he has promised to me. I cannot say what makes me believe that is true. I have had no blinding revelations on my road to Damascus. All I have had are many times of doubt, or worse still, times when I have put all thoughts of my faith out of my mind as being too big and worrying to think about because it got in the way of my living my life.

I am not very good at 'praying', and I am certainly not a 'vocal' missionary. I try to live the life that I think Christ would have wanted me to live, but I do not often think that I have come anywhere near the 'pass mark'. The Church is my College in the quest for learning, and the Scriptures are my text book. Sadly, like students in many other spheres, my text book is too often hidden in the desk, and my attention in class easily wavers. Somehow, though, my faith still stays with me.

————————————————

& As a child and young person my faith was principally influenced by my mother's strong Catholic faith but, unfortunately, during this time we had a major problem with our parish priest which tested the faith of all the family to the limit. Although I attended a Catholic secondary school, where we had weekly Mass and religious instruction, I do not recall this as being a major influence on my faith.

At approximately the same time that I left school to go to university, my mother after much heart searching left the Catholic faith and became a Quaker. Although I attended the RC chaplaincy during most of this period, none of my friends were catholics and my faith definitely weakened. It was only when I returned to university several years later as a postgraduate student that I became more involved with the chaplaincy and in founding and running a new Catholic Graduate Society. By meeting regularly with others with a strong faith and being involved with them in planning and organising meetings and other activities my faith was certainly nourished during this second period at university.

When working in New Zealand, I was fortunate to discover very quickly a small but very lively Catholic community at a small church in the city centre. My faith was nourished over many years by associating with this group and seeing the way that the lives of some of the individuals were influenced by their faith. In addition to attending Mass there regularly, both on Sundays and weekdays, I was involved in many other activities such as regular discussion groups and several weekend retreats all of which were important to my faith. I was also strongly influenced by the priest, a man of deep personal faith. My own faith was further nourished by seeing the strong faith of some of the young people in the chaplaincy, as well as a small group of older people who regularly attended Mass there.

I have relatively recently returned to England. Despite attending Mass regularly, I have not yet become much involved in parish life and feel that the priests do not encourage active involvement by the parishioners. However, my faith is nourished by seeing the strong faith of my sister and her husband and many other people in the parish who often attend daily Mass and are involved in other activities such as prayer groups, despite the lack of encouragement.

Of course there are many other factors which nourish my faith, particularly regular Mass and Holy Communion as well as personal prayer and reading about the faith. However, it is undoubtedly associating with others with a strong faith which has had the greatest influence in nourishing my own faith.

As a cradle Catholic, I tend to take my faith for granted, and I have never really considered what it is that makes it such a strong force in my life.

I could start with Sunday sermons. From time to time I am inspired by what I hear and I take the message home with me and I feel that it all makes sense. Sometimes I get a better understanding of a gospel reading and its relevance to my everyday life. There have been times too when I have actually changed the way I acted as a result of what I have heard.

However, my faith is nourished much more by the actions of other people: friends who live their lives just the way Jesus did, caring, sharing and loving. They are always there whenever needed and I doubt if they would ever let me down, yet they expect no reward or even thanks for what they do. They are totally dependable and true Christians in every sense of the word.

My faith is also nourished by my job. I teach young children who can be so spontaneous and trusting in their approach to God. They have no inhibitions and talk to God in a most natural and easy manner using their own words. On many occasions I have felt a sudden upsurge in my faith after listening to the children's own prayers. I think we can all learn a lot from listening to and watching young children.

Lastly my faith is nourished through my own children. Though they are grown up now, I can stand back and feel pleased with the way they have turned out. They are caring, considerate, human beings, despite leading busy lives, and I feel this is in part due to their Catholic upbringing. When I reflect on this, my faith is strengthened and I am extremely grateful.

☙   In thinking of how my faith as a Catholic is nourished in the present, I recognise how much is due to the gift of faith received and nourished in the past, which is still a continuing influence in the present.

My sister and I were brought up in a Catholic family in which we were nourished by prayer. I heard faith-filled words, such as 'Thank God for my cup of tea' and gratitude to God was frequently expressed. We said grace before and after meals, we prayed the Rosary and other prayers, and were encouraged in devotion to the Saints and reading their lives. We received the Sacraments in the parish, and these were always primary sources of nourishment. I was baptised at nine days old. We attended weekly Sunday school, went to Confession, to Mass, and received the treasure of Holy Communion; we were confirmed, took part in outdoor processions and went to Benediction. Other memorable influences were the Catholic primary and secondary schools we attended. I recall how we learnt the whole of St. Mark's Gospel by heart (I carried it in my pocket) - and we learned so much of the love and life of Jesus, and of the faith generally.

When in adult life I became engaged, my fiancé, after previously receiving instruction from Anglican, Congregational, and Catholic ministers, was baptised and received into the Catholic Church. This was a source of great blessing and joy, and our practice of the faith together has been a great source of nourishment. We both became speakers in the Catholic Evidence Guild, which was a nourishing experience for many years. After study and prayer, we spoke on outdoor platforms, and were encouraged to regard this as an appointment with the Holy Spirit, on whom we relied for courage, for love of all who came to listen or heckle, and for inspiration. We were encouraged to spend as much time in prayer before the Blessed Sacrament as we did on the outdoor platform, if this were possible, and other Guild members present would be praying. Speaking at Tower Hill I felt close to St Thomas More, near the place of his martyrdom, and asked for his intercession.

Belonging to a prayer group has also been a great spiritual help and nourishment. Sharing in prayer, hymns, Bible readings, hearing the experiences of others in the group, and being moved by their deep love and prayer life, was enriching for us both. I am now attending a new prayer group which has been formed in my parish.

Other ways of spiritual nourishment have been pilgrimages, especially to Lourdes, and most memorably to the Holy Land - a wonderful experience of prayer and so moving to be in the places where Jesus lived and worked. I am nourished by daily Mass and daily Bible reading, by meditation, praying the Divine Office daily (and being aware of unity with others throughout the world), by music and hymns, spiritual writings, homilies, talks, retreats, involvement in catechetical work to all ages, belonging to various Catholic organisations, and having the great privilege of being a Reader and Minister of Holy Communion.

Sadly for us, my husband died two years ago, yet my faith gives assurance of eternal dwelling in heaven and of our continuing love and prayer to unite us.

'See what the love the Father has given us' (1 John 3:1). It is the thought of God's infinite love for all people; the love of the Father, Son and Holy Spirit, which nourishes me above all; and God's forgiving love which pardons me and sets me free from all my sins, failures and shortcomings. His love is reflected in so many holy people and I am grateful for them all, and nourished by them.

Russian Orthodox

It is not easy for an Orthodox to separate 'spirituality' from the rest of our life in Christ, but as a convert who spent 40 years as an Anglican, I could mention a few things that have made a deep—and exciting—impression on me.

It came as a great relief for me to stand in a service and see people making their confessions in church—in the open, before an icon of Christ, with the priest standing at the side as a friend and witness. To watch them kneeling to receive forgiveness and then walking away, often in tears, made me realise that 'yes! the Church is a company of forgiven sinners, not a body of self-righteous saints, and the church building is a place where one comes not to be on one's best behaviour but to reveal the very worst things about oneself, **and yet still be loved**'. This was a real revelation.

I came to appreciate the way Orthodoxy is lived out in the home situation, where things like prayers before the icons and an Orthodox attitude to bodily participation through fasting and feasting makes worship an integral part of daily life.

I appreciated Orthodox worship as heaven on earth, and the fact that it is not designed to be man- or woman-centred, but God-centred. As we enter the church we step into God's realm. But this is not in any sense escapism but a home-coming into the eternal now, into the presence of the Trinity. And this enables me to go back into the world and try to bring that experience of heaven to others.

I was impressed by the awareness of the Holy Spirit at the centre of the Church - in the sacraments and the services as well as in individuals. But this transparency to the Spirit is understood in much deeper terms than expressing outward gifts; it is a fundamental indwelling of the Spirit himself as Gift; and the struggle to open oneself more and more to this indwelling and to become all love is revealed as the essence of the Christian life.

This could all be summed up in the word 'participation'. This is made especially obvious during Holy Week, when we really feel we live the

experience day by day during our very long services (some last more than
three hours). By Good Friday we are, in a small way, exhausted, hungry and
spiritually aware of the horror of the Passion. We face and live through
something of the frightening wonder of a God, who has been crucified by us
humans, all of us—and whose response is unimaginable, saving love.

Yes, I find the music, the icons and the incense personally conducive to
worship, but these are only a part of a much deeper whole which centres on
the truth of the Easter message: Christ is risen, and calls us to follow him via
Calvary to the Resurrection.

URC

⊗   Being nourished spiritually is, I think, like being nourished physically. Just as there are many components to a good, balanced diet, so there are many aspects of the spiritual life, if we are to be properly nourished in our Christian walk of faith. My personal experiences of this will, I am sure, echo these of every other Christian, and so we are all brought together as we seek to live our lives on a spiritual basis.

The Bible has always been a source of wonder and fascination for me, and 'my' Bible for the last thirty years has been the *New English Bible.* I value other translations, of course, but 'my' version bears witness to the countless times I have been challenged, taught, strengthened, comforted and inspired, because there are underlining, personal comments, and cross references throughout its pages. It really is to me God's Word, and this is where He so often speaks to me, as the Holy Spirit guides and reveals.

Prayer can grow out of Bible reading and study, either immediately or at later times, solitary prayer, or shared with my husband; prayer in its many varieties as I go about my daily life and work. Some years ago I was greatly moved during a prayer counselling school, when I heard, for the first time, people singing in the Spirit. When I commented on this afterwards prayers were offered for me also to receive the gift of tongues. Nothing happened then, and I just accepted that as being not quite the thing for a URC elder! However, a fortnight later I was indeed blessed by this gift, in a quiet time, on my own, at home, and it was such a wonderful revelation to me of the truth that the Holy Spirit at work in the life of the early church is still active in the same way today. This has been a gift, which has nourished me personally, and which has also sometimes been used as a blessing and an active ingredient when I pray for others one-to-one.

I find spiritual nourishment, too, in the many traditions of prayer that have come to us through the ages, the medieval saints, the Celtic, the Catholic, the Jewish and so on – each of them opening up new paths and experiences and disciplines.

And what of the times of corporate worship with fellow Christians, Sunday-by-Sunday? The sacraments, the services and festivals, the sermons? I am privileged to be closely involved in a music group and a singing group, and the ministry of healing, both public and private. What spiritual strengthening is there, in so many different forms! What nourishment is there, in the starting of Christian fellowship and friendship, not only in my own church but also in churches of other denominations, as we worship together once a month, in small groups and in large!

Jesus, 'the Bread of Life', the source of 'Living Waters' is our greatest giver of spiritual nourishment. May we always give him thanks and praise.

ℒ   I believe that there are two different emphases here. Nourishment in the faith implies education and is necessarily largely church-derived, whereas spiritual nourishment implies a sustaining of spirituality (probably with an educational element) which may largely come from outside the church – whether 'the church' is defined as the place where one worships, or the denomination within which one worships, or the Holy Catholic Church.

The nourishment of education is of course also continuous. In my case this was begun by Christian parents, and included Sunday School in a Congregational Church, and school worship (I can't say I got anything at all out of 'scripture' lessons, though, except an idea of the geography of the missionary journeys of Paul). My spiritual nourishment has continued by good preaching and teaching in church services, by reading, and by insights from radio (occasionally even television). Quite important is my participation in the Congregational or United Reformed Church monthly church meeting (in a succession of churches) where I have often been enlightened by hearing other members' views and by intelligent discussion. Although I have attended house groups I have not found them a source of intellectual light and truth – rather a useful exercise in community and a practical expression of love.

On both counts—education and sustaining spirituality—collective worship is very important to me. Like many, I find solitary prayer difficult; I did get off on the wrong foot thinking that anything addressed to God should be perfectly expressed, and in accurate 1662 English; but I believe that prayer is essential and group prayer a vital task of the church. I listen whenever I can to the Radio 4 Daily Service and I usually hear the broadcast service before setting off for church on a Sunday morning. I find almost all worship uplifting, never mind what the denomination or style.

My greatest spiritual sustenance, however, comes from beauty. First of all the created world (and though I say solitary prayer is difficult, the communion with God in rejoicing over beauty and giving thanks for it, in instant, often wordless, prayers, punctuates my day). I also find God and spiritual truth in painting, music and poetry—most of all in poetry, which is my natural medium.

In my teenage years, my receiving nurture from the church was problematic; I was deeply alienated from the church by the non-inclusive language and attitudes it had in the 1940s and 1950s (growing up as I was in a family where boy and girl were equally valued), and by its almost total lack of interest in the beauty which was my profound concern. I used to sit in church looking at the text lettered round the central arch, WORSHIP THE LORD IN THE BEAUTY OF HOLINESS, and thinking 'fine – but what about worship in the holiness of beauty?' It took me a long time to come to any sense of the church as a spiritual home; even now I sometimes feel a stranger, although I know I am there sustained by a world of love – mine to give as much as to receive. This love is most fully expressed in the Communion service – the very centre of the church's spirituality, its holiness and its caritas.

Ultimately God godself is our spiritual nourishment, and if blocked in one way may communicate in another. As the recalcitrant teenager already mentioned, the knowledge of the presence and joy of God swept me off my feet; I walk in that light.

Bodies in Association

*write about spiritual nourishment
at the heart of their particular organisation*

Association of Interchurch Families (AIF)

Seeking God together

Interchurch family spirituality focuses on marriage and unity. The close link between these was affirmed by Pope John Paul II in the words he addressed to interchurch families when he visited Britain in 1982. Speaking at York during a celebration of marriage and family life, he spoke directly to partners in mixed marriages between baptised Christians, one of whom was a Roman Catholic:

'You live in your marriage the hopes and the difficulties of the path to Christian unity. Express that hope in prayer together, in the unity of love. Together invite the Holy Spirit into your hearts and into your homes. He will help you to grow in trust and understanding.'

Interchurch families share their relationship and experience in daily life across church boundaries. In this respect they are the smallest of ecumenical partnerships.

Sacraments

United through the sacraments of baptism and marriage, many partners in interchurch families believe they share the same faith and belong to the one Church of Christ, although this is at present divided. Searching for God's will is a continuous dialogue in their marriage and family life. The experience is often frustrating and painful, but can also be challenging and joyful.

Sharing in the sacraments is of great significance for interchurch families. It is hurtful when couples are unable to share the eucharist, which above all is the sacrament of peace, unity and reconciliation. Children may see this inability to share as a sign of disunity, particularly poignant when their parents are trying to bring them up as Christians.

The domestic church

Interchurch family spirituality is not an individual spirituality. When Christians from different denominations marry, they have a wonderful opportunity to share their two spiritual traditions with each other and with their children.

The domestic church is particularly important for interchurch families. The diversity of their backgrounds enriches their relationship. Love helps them overcome problems. It enhances their sense of unity in a way that helps them see their differences as gifts to be shared rather than obstacles to be overcome. The search for God in the diversity of their experience provides an insight into ways in which the churches might draw closer together.

Interchurch families may feel a strong sense of double belonging and be involved in the lives of both their churches at many different levels, but all of them are likely to feel at least some degree of tension in their marriage and family life. One problem is that they experience a fuller communion with each other than do the Churches they represent. Interchurch couples share the joys, hopes, fears and anxieties of all married partners. But for interchurch partners, to the love and oneness they experience in the mystery of sacramental marriage is added this further dimension, of being at one with each other across church divisions – unity and marriage hand in hand.

Our spiritual treasure

This pilgrimage involves a loving commitment which can never be satisfied with partial communion between the churches. It will always mean engaging in dialogue in the quest for spiritual union. It may sometimes mean going beyond the conventions. It will always mean trusting, hoping and waiting on God through the unity of the Father, Son and Holy Spirit. The tension can be hurtful, but it is a meaningful tension, which carries within it a real hope of reconciliation and unity.

This is a spirituality of love and experience – a spirituality from below rather than from above.   Perhaps this is the spiritual treasure interchurch families can offer the churches.   Certainly this spirituality exemplifies the importance of relationships in the search for church unity.   It is reflection upon real experience from the point of view of faith.   Interpersonal relationships and a true dialogue, which recognises that unity emerges through diversity, are the essence of this spirituality.

Being an interchurch family is what their spirituality is about. 'Unity is both the journey's end and the way of journeying now.' (CTE Forum report, 1997)

Bible Society

The spiritual nourishment provided by Bible Society unsurprisingly leans heavily, but not exclusively, towards the availability and use of the Bible. Account also needs to be taken of the efforts for provision within the Society as well as its work outside.

Staff nurture

Within Bible Society there are prayers occurring three times daily, using an office and readings developed in partnership with the Northumbria Community. There is also a monthly worship service with a variety of internal and external speakers.

For employees, access to a Bible, whether in print or on tape, is not a problem!

Resourcing Churches

This availability is also offered as part of a range of services to help the spiritual nourishment of churches. Copies of many translations, including the new *Contemporary English Version*, can be bought singly or in bulk quite reasonably. The *Faith Comes By Hearing* project offers a structured programme for congregations to listen to the New Testament.

The Bible in TransMission magazine is produced to provide stimulation and encouragement to ministers and leaders, while the *Open Book Bible Experience* provides exploration of the Bible in thought-provoking and creative ways.

In conjunction with the Northumbria Community's *Telling Place* there is a storytelling project aimed at helping people engage biblical truth through experiencing stories. *Reel Issues*, developed by Ian Maher of the Church Army, enables biblical themes to be gleaned, discussed and applied through mainstream cinema films. Local Action Groups provide the encouragement of a worldwide view and specific focus for what God is doing through the Bible. A

Bible Sunday pack is released annually to help congregations focus in their worship on the Bible and its powerful effect.

Research

Fuelling all this is ongoing research into how people use the Bible, consultations on Hermeneutics, and Education projects aimed at making Religious Education in schools more effective.

Through these and other activities, Bible Society seeks to nourish the spirituality of its own staff, the churches in England and Wales, and indeed the nation, by opening the Book to the people and the people to the Book.

CHAD (Church Action on Disability)

Relevance of the parable of the Good Samaritan

CHAD's contribution to the spirituality of Christian people in England is one which challenges and calls all people to a commitment to the Gospel of 'social holiness', specifically in relation to disabled people. The story of the Good Samaritan helps to demonstrate this point. CHAD frequently receives letters from people who are disabled, describing their experiences in churches. From these experiences it is possible to draw parallels between the actions of some churches and the consequent experiences of many disabled people, and the robbers and the man who is beaten by them. Many disabled people's experiences include being ignored in churches, being asked to leave because they are too disruptive to the traditional way of doing things, being made to feel worthless because of an assumption that disabled people are not able to contribute in any way to a church's life and worship and, on occasion, being described as faithless, when attempts to physically "heal" a disabled person have been in vain. Disabled people have been left broken and marginalised by many churches and then abandoned at 'the side of the road'. Of course this is not always the case but these negative experiences are much more common than positive experiences.

Transformation

CHAD, therefore, challenges churches to be transformed into places of holiness. The story of the Good Samaritan gives us two examples of holiness. The first is that demonstrated by the Priest and the Levite, both of whom are so conscious of the importance of ritual purity - a mark of holiness - that they are not prepared to help the beaten man who lies wounded on the roadside. The second example of holiness is that shown by the Good Samaritan himself, and it is this type of holiness which CHAD challenges the churches to embrace. For it is a holiness which is prepared to take imaginative risks for the sake of disabled people, a holiness prepared to be disrupted in order to be inclusive and prepared to act in a way which enables disabled people to participate fully in the life of church communities at local, national and international levels, whatever the cost.

The gift of the marginalised

Finally, it is reasonable to consider that churches also have experiences like those of the beaten man. Church communities are wounded not only because they are made up of broken people, but because of the ways in which churches are increasingly the objects of criticism in society. In this context the roles of churches and disabled people can be reversed, because disabled people also have the capacity to be Good Samaritans and to live lives of holiness. The Good Samaritan himself was on the margins of the community to which the beaten man belonged, but it was this person on the margins which helped the beaten man to recover to the fullness of life.

CHAD challenges Christian communities to a life of holiness which is not afraid to act for the sake of justice and inclusion. It asks churches to be still and silent so that they can be open to the contributions which many of its marginalised members can make. This mixture of active and passive dimensions to holiness calls for mutuality, trust and respect between disabled and non-disabled members of churches, and it is this spirit of holiness which CHAD challenges Christ's church to embrace.

Christians Aware

Christians Aware grew and developed entirely on the shoulders of committed, active members who, for years, have been supporting the organisation in many ways by spreading the word, fund-raising or just by participating in the various events. It is no bad thing sometimes to stop and think why people joined a particular organisation and what it was that drew them to it. More to the point, to ask why they are still there? What do they get out of it?

Celebrating difference and diversity

Regional Representatives recently shared their personal responses to these questions. Some said they are drawn to Christians Aware because it values experiences abroad. Many of our members have been to various parts of the world to live or to work, and this may have been a turning point in their lives. When they return, they feel they need to take these experiences further, to talk about and share them with others, and perhaps get other people interested and involved. On the whole, they want to make good use of experiences which have, in some cases, changed their lives. For them, Christians Aware is the channel through which they have the opportunity to satisfy their need.

Christians Aware believes in celebrating difference, creativity and diversity. In a world where being different or belonging to a minority group is a reason for being excluded, ostracised, or persecuted, Christians Aware not only accepts but celebrates difference and diversity and recognises that there is a lot to learn and to enrich lives from other groups and other cultures. Christians Aware also recognises and encourages creative self-expression, and gives an opportunity for people to use and develop their talents. Is it not our duty and mission as Christians not to bury our 'talents' but to use them to the full?

The real world

It is this rich mine of cultures and experiences that draws some people to Christians Aware. They discover and revel in other cultures, in having a window onto the real world as real people see it and experience it, rather than the glossy pictures given by governments, tourist boards and travel agents. Christians Aware provides a great opportunity to meet people, and make long-lasting friendships. Through knowing the people we also get to know their concerns and their problems and the issues that are important to them. In this 'global village' called Planet Earth, we need to be aware of the role we as individuals and nations play in each other's lives and the repercussions of an action taken by a group at one side of the globe on another group at the other side. The knowledge of the reality of the issues and the people who suffer urges us to take action, for who likes to hurt their friend knowingly?

Listening

The learning starts with listening, for Christians Aware listens! Many people talk but not many people listen. Listening shows caring, and this draws some people into the group. Caring drives us into action and also into prayer, and some find the regular prayer pointers very moving. Christians Aware believes in the power of prayer and action simultaneously.

The courage to grapple with issues that others fear, the openness, the diversity, the cultural and spiritual exchange and stimulation, meeting God through His world and His people, working for Justice and Peace, all this and more makes Christians Aware unique for its members. The books, conferences, work-camps, visits, cards, and concerts, mean a lot more now than mere 'recreational activities'; they are a need, a mission, a way of life.

When I asked my questions of those sitting around the table at the Regional Representatives' meeting, I did not know what to expect, but one part of me thought it would be an interesting exercise and a revealing one too. When organisations and churches are complaining about the lack of commitment and the people are complaining about the lack of spiritual fulfilment in their lives and activities, it was very uplifting to hear a dozen people talk with such feeling about 'a hobby'! What I got was this torrent of genuine, sincere emotion. I have to admit I was moved by what I heard during the short brainstorm. It was a learning experience for me personally, and I learnt more about my friends.

The College of Preachers

Encouragement

A participant in our recent major conference, 'Preaching Christ for a new Millennium', commented that the event had 'changed her life'. The comment illustrates that the College offers not only practical help and instruction in the work of preaching, but exercises (for some) a profound ministry of encouragement.

Such encouragement is likely to come in the form of the affirmation of people's preaching ministry at a time when the validity of preaching is widely questioned, in church circles as well as beyond. In the case of this conference, as in many other smaller events staffed by the College, it may well also have come in a very personal way, as individuals had opportunity in a safe environment to preach a sermon and receive constructive feedback.

Spiritual nurture

The hope, of course, is that through the ministry we exercise among preachers, the church at large will benefit spiritually. We believe in the central importance of the ministry of the word for the building up of believers and the conversion of unbelievers. But if the ministers themselves are not resourced and ministered to, there will be a dearth of life in that word 'ministry' and thus a paucity of effect in the church generally.

There are particular ways in which issues of spirituality feed into current thinking about preaching, and in which spiritually-sensitive preaching can serve people's growth in faith. For example, preachers are learning to apply the tools offered by the Myers-Briggs Personality Type Indicator to their self-understanding and in their appreciation of the variety of ways in which a congregation hears and responds to a sermon according to personality preferences. Work has been going on in the area of gender and preaching. There has been an upsurge of interest in the imaginative dimensions of preaching - emphasising that it does not have to be a purely cerebral, rationalistic exercise. In all these ways many preachers are being liberated to 'be themselves' in Christ and that should certainly in due course have a knock-on liberating effect on congregations. The College does all it can to encourage this process.

Empowerment

Another trend the College wishes to nurture is the view of preaching as a corporate rather than a solo act. Even if only one person actually gives voice to the word, it should be a word that emerges from a process of listening not only to Scripture but also to the congregation, the community and the world. The preacher speaks not only *to* the congregation but, in an important sense, *for* the congregation. Practically, this philosophy should lead to an increase in group times of listening to God - in preparing sermons with the preacher, and in reflecting on them afterwards. The fundamental spiritual effect of this should be a new empowerment of the people of God - as those who *together* hear the word of God and take it into the world.

The Focolare Movement

Twenty-four-hours-a-day faith

On the day this was written two people came to our Focolare house in south London and each was asked how they felt the Focolare spirituality nourished them. One said, 'It made my faith become a 24-hours-a-day thing' and 'it is so helpful to meet with others regularly to share our experiences of trying to live out our Christian lives'. The other said, 'It helped me to bridge the gap between Sunday and all the other days of the week and to understand the importance of being united with God and with one another by living the Gospel'.

Love

For all members of the Focolare the bedrock on which their spiritual life is built is belief in God's immense love for them. From this comes their response to put God first in their lives, before everything else, and then to love other people as a consequence. They cannot remain indifferent to God's love and so they want to love him as Jesus did by doing his will, 'My food is to do the will of my Father'. God's will is to be found in Scripture. Focolare members try to re-evangelise their way of thinking and loving by living out the words of the Gospel. A useful way of doing this is through the *Word of Life* leaflet (15,000 of which are printed in the UK each month). Through living out words of Scripture, such as 'Whatever you do to the least you do to me', they make the discovery of the presence of Jesus in each neighbour, and what was frequently an apathetic faith becomes dynamic. Focolare members seek to love with charity, the love that comes from God and which makes them see Christ in each person. This charity always takes the initiative and makes them love others as themselves, making them one with brothers and sisters in sufferings and in joys.

But Jesus said 'Love one another as I have loved you', and this is the measure of love that members of Focolare feel called to live in their everyday lives. It is the root of all they do.

Scripture

Particular words of Scripture are considered as 'pillars' of the spirituality of the Focolare. One of these is the cry of Jesus on the cross, 'My God, my God, why have you forsaken me?' Sufferings, especially those concerning disunity, are seen as aspects of his suffering and therefore opportunities to love him. Looking at Jesus, people find the strength to continue loving even when it becomes particularly difficult.

Another pillar is the presence of Christ amongst those who are united: 'Where two or more are gathered together in my name there am I in the midst of them'. These two sentences from the Gospel are fundamental to the ecumenism promoted by the Focolare .

St Teresa of Avila spoke of building the 'interior castle' of individual spirituality. The Focolare Movement, while recognising the importance of a personal choice of God and a relationship with him, sees this in relation to love of neighbour and mutual love. Hence the building up of the 'exterior castle', where Christ is present amongst his people.

Practice

In practical terms groups meet regularly, on a weekly or monthly basis, and seek to have the presence of Christ amongst them through mutual love. Here experiences of putting the Gospel into practice are shared and the presence of Christ brings light and strength into many situations, enabling people to persevere in loving, and bring about real changes in relationships and circumstances. There are courses of formation in spirituality at the Focolare Centre for Unity in Welwyn Garden City, and *New City* magazine is another useful element in formation and nourishment.

What has been said above does not cover the whole spirituality, which nourishes an indefinable number of people throughout the world. Other aspects of Gospel life, such as the Eucharist, the Church, the Holy Spirit, and Mary are also very important. The spirituality is like a compendium making Scripture alive in each moment.   It is this living of the Word together that makes a difference in the life of members of Focolare and gives them encouragement and enthusiasm to go ahead.

The Iona Community

Ways of being and ways of doing

As members of the Iona Community we are committed to a five-fold Rule:

- ❖ Daily prayer and Bible-reading
- ❖ Sharing and accounting for the use of our money
- ❖ Sharing and accounting for the use of our time
- ❖ Action for justice and peace in society
- ❖ Meeting with and accounting to each other.

This Rule is lived out in our daily lives, wherever we are. Every aspect of the Rule has a spiritual dimension. There is no official Iona Community 'line' on spirituality, but it could generally be said that our spirituality is engaged in the concerns of the world, so that our commitment to justice and peacemaking and our personal devotional discipline are inextricably linked. Thus we try to live an integrated spirituality which is more about an attitude, a way of life, a process than about any particular religious practice. A fundamental philosophy of the Iona Community is that work and worship co-exist, nourishing and undergirding each other. As an illustration of this, on the island of Iona, at the end of morning worship, we remain standing after the closing responses to move straight out into the work of the day, only sharing the blessing together at the end of the day at evening worship.

Most of the 240 members, however, do not live on Iona but live and work and worship in towns, cities and villages throughout Britain and Ireland, and beyond. Members of the Community are also members of local churches of all denominations. Here is what some members say about spiritual nourishment:

'As an activist I needed the reflective side and this was nourished by the Iona Community – meeting people has also nourished this side of me.'

'The challenge to us is in the Rule – it is a way of holding together the different aspects of all of life. The Iona Community has been better at nurturing the active rather than the reflective side of me.'

'I have a very lonely spirituality – nature is a great source of wonder and detachment. I feel I'm an outsider to things, but I have a deep desire to be included. I have a real need to be part of a tradition. The Abbey (on Iona) and the island offer that. The Community holds my anarchism – I don't have to compromise my beliefs to be part of it.'

'My spirituality comes in fits and starts—not terribly organised. It comes in moments of quietness, mystery or even fear. There is something in the dark hole of the well, or the cliff edge, which confronts me with deep and powerful things within myself and beyond... Spirituality is about the 'ahaa' moments: of sudden realisation through thinking, talking, reading... Moments of real spirituality are when I go deep within myself.'

'I'm interested in a spirituality of the everyday. I tend to shy away from anything that's trying to organise my spirituality.'

'There are moments on a Sunday morning when we (on Iona) are singing a Wild Goose song and I get a real boost.'

'One of the things that helps me to grow is the conversations that we have (as members) that are challenging, supporting and enriching all at once.'

'When I visit my Roman Catholic friend in Manchester I encounter a place of centering and peace – couldn't we have more of these places?'

'Iona is a place that gives me something, particularly in the worship when I am there.'

'The agenda for the Iona Community comes from the world, not from the church. The church is there to respond to the agenda of the world. The Iona Community helps me to keep pushing forward.'

'Spirituality is about ways of being and ways of doing.'

We recommend three books for readers who might want to learn about the spirituality of the Iona Community:

Ron Ferguson, *Chasing the Wild Goose,* Wild Goose Publications, 1998.

Ruth Harvey (ed.), *Wrestling and Resting,* CTBI, 1999 .

Norman Shanks, *Iona – God's Energy: the spirituality and vision of the Iona Community,* Hodder & Stoughton, 1999.

L'Arche

Community Households

L'Arche (which means The Ark) is an International network of 120 Christian Communities where people with and without learning disabilities live and work together.

The Communities are made up of Community Households, where we live together sharing the ordinary things of life: shopping, cooking, eating, cleaning and praying. Many Communities also have workshops where high quality craft work is done by the people with learning disabilities.

Gospel values

Our Communities' values are rooted in the gospels, and especially in the vision of God's Kingdom described by Jesus in the beatitudes. In L'Arche it is the outsider, the disabled, the vulnerable, the powerless and the degraded who reveal the face of God. In L'Arche we discover that we are all equal in the eyes of God; equally broken, equally loved. Our society does not deal with difference and with weakness well. We are all seeking to be strong, to be powerful and to be beautiful. This search is often an attempt to flee the unspoken and terrifying awareness of our vulnerability. In L'Arche we meet this vulnerability unhidden and un-denied. People with learning disabilities have often suffered much and have been deeply wounded. They have known loss and rejection, and they may live their suffering very openly. In living alongside this suffering, we encounter our own wounds, acknowledged and unacknowledged.

Ecumenical sharing

In Britain our Communities are ecumenical. We share our lives together as members of many different churches and denominations. This gives the opportunity for learning about the gifts of churches different from our own. It also means living with the pain of disunity. The Community that we can share at our meal tables is uncomfortably mirrored by our division at the Eucharist.

Our experience

In the experience of living Community and of making a commitment to a group of people, all as broken and as loved as each other, we discover something of the healing promised by Jesus in the Beatitudes: not a nice, easy, uncomplicated healing, but healing rooted in our vulnerability and in the mess of life. In L'Arche we have discovered that those that society has rejected have much to teach us: not about how to be strong, how to become better or how to be powerful, but about how to live and to love.

These lessons are taught by Sylvia, standing at the door of our Community household to greet you, as if she has known you forever, although she has just met you for the first time; by Jean as she tells you that she missed you, although you have only been away for the afternoon; by Philip, who faithfully remembers the birthdays of every Community member, as you open the card he sent. In L'Arche we learn together in the ordinary things of life, and we are taught by unexpected teachers.

Retreat Association

The role of a retreat

'Going on retreat is a time to let the weeds grow,' I was told at Bath University Chaplaincy recently. For the speaker, going on a retreat was the equivalent of rest. In a fallow time comes refreshment. It sounds good, but ...

'Retreats are when we are left with God and nothing else. It's a dangerous place'. Within hours of listening to the speaker at the university I am being told this. My conversationalist is now a giver of retreats. This definition is more alarming and yet paradoxically more attractive, at least if you go by the number of people seeking opportunities to go on retreat these days.

The local congregation still provides a spiritual home for some. But for many it is too set in doctrines and patterns that cannot respond to the often hesitant, short-term, issue-based world of today's spiritual pilgrim. The Retreat Association office in Bermondsey is never busier than when a national paper runs a feature on retreats, and such enquirers invariably wish to sit light to Christian belief or are Christians who need to be at a distance from church structures.

Those involved with retreats are finding that they are increasingly asked to respond to these concerns. Here is one paradox. The spiritual search of this time that does not wish to be religious is constantly knocking on the door of the religious. There is a desire to sample but not belong.

The theme of one Retreat Association Conference was 'Crossing thresholds!' One conference member wrote 'the role of a retreat is to enable a person to discover with God the thresholds and barriers in their life and with that discovery the courage to cross or dismantle them.' Here is a spirituality of engagement that many in the retreat movement willingly embrace.

At the tenth anniversary celebration of the Retreat Association the words of Michael Ramsay in 1969 were recalled as having the tone of a prophecy whose time has come. *'Retreat will become less a thing apart. In a sense more secular. It will be more than ever clear that the self which goes into retreat is the real self that is a part of the world, the self that can't escape from the world. When I go into retreat God's impact upon me as a self will not be upon myself as a kind of pious thing abstracted from the world. It will be more than ever the self of everyday existence.'*

Integrity

This call to integrity is important. One of the dangers of this current fascination with retreats is that it will reinforce the fashion for individual fulfilment. Spiritual tourists seeking the next package deal from the latest guru or spiritual hot spot can be as self-seeking as those who holiday in safe tourist zones and never see the real countryside. People in the retreat movement are not blind to this and acknowledge its seductive power. For running counter to this often rampant individualism is another feature of today's God-search complexity - the desire for community. This is more than a need to feel part of some thing. There is a search for a community of meaning. Here again is paradox! On the one hand both from within and beyond the church there is a wariness of becoming religiously shaped and structured. Provide the appropriate space for people to move beyond the beliefs and dogma of their tradition and all sorts of hesitations and deeply felt questions emerge. Counter to the culture of those Christians who deal in affirmation and certainties run those for whom a doctrinal response to Christ is not their way. This can be a lonely place to find oneself.

Movement into community

On the other hand, these isolated individuals seek a more authentic source of community. The Retreat Association is seen by some to be such a community, but they recoil from its structure of being an association of denominational groups. Others may become part of the tertiary orders of traditional religious communities or associates of contemporary communities such as Northumbria, Iona or Corrymeela. The latter three, although very clearly different, have in common the characteristic of being a dispersed movement. They provide a point of identity and relationship, a gathering space where people can align themselves with certain priorities. This movement into community, community based on loyalty to a chosen common need, may be the shape of tomorrow's church. The Retreat Association may be contributing to the formation of the future church but all we can ever be is a watcher of the acts of God among us.

SCM (Student Christian Movement)

Openness and inclusivity

SCM has sometimes been jokingly referred to as 'The Slightly Christian Movement' by those who maybe think that the spiritual element of the Movement has, at times, been somewhat neglected! Maintaining a balance between our commitment both to social justice issues and to the spiritual growth of our members is an ongoing concern within SCM circles. Our underlying ethos is one of openness and inclusivity. Consequently our members come from all kinds of backgrounds and include those on the fringes of Christian circles as well as those who claim to have no faith but are, nevertheless, keen to explore religious and social justice issues. Operating in such a broad and open context requires some discipline so as not to lose sight of the basic aims of the Movement.

Resources

SCM seeks to provide spiritual nourishment for Christian students in several ways. Our publications examine often controversial and difficult contemporary issues, such as Clause 28, images of Christ or disability. We hope to challenge people to wrestle with the big questions (whether that is a comfortable experience or not) and to debate them in an environment in which all opinions are respected, rather than ignoring complex issues or brushing them safely under the carpet. We don't provide a nice, tidy set of answers to these questions but we do offer resources as an aid to the exploration. We believe that this process is vital for our faith to be alive, dynamic and relevant to society today.

As well as publications, SCM organises events (often in collaboration with the Catholic Student Council) which bring together students from all parts of the country and from different denominations. These weekends offer a rare opportunity for Anglican, Catholic and Free Church students to spend a weekend exploring together a theme and, just as importantly, to spend time chatting with each other, exchanging opinions and ideas, and making new friendships with people they might not otherwise mix with. Recent conferences have been on themes such as the Beatitudes and the Taizé Community. People usually leave these events feeling inspired and, somehow, more deeply connected with the wider Christian student community.

Worship

Worship is an important part of these gatherings and is often led by the students themselves. Planning the worship for ecumenical meetings presents a real challenge if we are trying to appeal to and include everyone and offend no one. However, when it works well, people seem to be aware that they have been part of something special and, even if it is just for a brief moment, the barriers seem to fade away.

Integrity

It is encouraging to see that most SCM groups now include some time for worship even if the rest of the meeting is spent debating an issue. There seems to be a general consensus within SCM that our commitment to social justice ought to be bound up with the nurturing of our spiritual lives, if there is to be any integrity in what we are doing.

YMCA

The challenge

'A growing number of today's young people no longer experience them (the churches) as their spiritual home... A growing number of young people are or are becoming spiritually homeless. They often are not even aware of their personal form of spirituality. The needs of all these different people cannot be covered by one type of church activity or by one type of religious activity only. Their world views and their spirituality vary widely. Pluralism can never be answered by one response only...

What we need is a new plurality of forms of Christian spirituality. And what we need are Christian spiritual homes for the many spiritually homeless. How does the YMCA respond to the growing number of spiritually homeless young people? And do young people experience their YMCA as a spiritual home for them?'

(source: European Alliance of YMCAs)

Our beliefs

The YMCA aims to offer young people and their communities opportunities to develop in body, mind and spirit. Underpinning this mission are our beliefs that:

- human well-being has material, physical and spiritual elements;

- spirituality is a fundamental part of being human. It is about relationships with others and with God, and about the search for identity, meaning, purpose and values by which to live;

- whilst each person has the capacity to journey towards greater wholeness, the spiritual dimension of life is often unexplored, principally because of indifference towards or suspicion of organised religion.

Our response

With these beliefs in mind, we would offer a number of thoughts from our experience of spiritual development work:

- Physical, material and spiritual well-being are inter-related. For example, YMCA Sports and Fitness programmes aim to contribute to the holistic development of the individual, in terms of achievement, self-image and the ability to participate with others.

- Our youth work engages young people with issues of values, meaning and purpose through relationships with youth workers which are characterised by trust and confidence.

- YMCA workers often express a desire for resources to help them explore issues of spirituality with young people. The YMCA's most recent collection of resources, *Living inTENSIONally*, has been published in partnership with Frontier Youth Trust.

- We believe there is more to spirituality than meeting a personal need for a sense of fulfilment. Spiritual experience ought to shape our beliefs and influence how we live. Therefore we believe that spirituality needs to be encouraged and nurtured in ways that develop our capacity for reflection on experience which helps to develop personal meaning, values, and social vision.

- We believe that there is a corporate dimension to well-being; a healthy community is one where people feel they belong, care for one another, treat each other with respect, have something to give and something to receive, and can share in decision-making. So within each YMCA we are committed to the building up of communities that offer individuals the opportunity to develop and flourish.

- Volunteer participation is central to how the YMCA works—
  giving people the chance to give time to others. By giving to
  others, volunteers learn and grow themselves. Through
  volunteering and lay participation, the YMCA offers
  opportunities for people to explore and express Christian
  discipleship. Reflection days for staff and lay members alike
  encourage the exploration of the relationship between life,
  work and prayer.

Young Women's Christian Association (YWCA)

Foundation

The YWCA is rooted in Christianity. In 1855 the Prayer Union for young women was founded and, in the same year, a hostel for Florence Nightingale nurses was opened. The combination of these two forces led to their amalgamation in 1877 and the beginning of the YWCA. The spirit of love, hope and a sense of belonging to a Christian organisation formed the backbone of the Association.

Spiritual nourishment

In the past, there have been many prayer groups, Bible studies and the involvement of local churches to ensure a strong Christian support system for all those involved with the YWCA. As times change and the nature of our work changes to match, the YWCA will need to develop new support systems for continued spiritual nourishment.

Social Gospel

Today's vision for the YWCA is to work as 'a force for change for women who are facing discrimination and inequalities of all kinds'. This is carried out through the provision of 21 youth and community projects around the country. It is also reflected in policy work which aims to improve the lives of young women, giving them hope and opportunity.

Guiding principles

Recommendations made at a Spirituality workshop in 1998 ensured that 'Spiritual Dimension' was included as one of the five guiding principles for the new YWCA business plan. This plan was drawn up in 1999 following the YWCA's withdrawal from social housing. It states that the YWCA will work from its Christian value base to ensure a recognition of the spiritual perspective of the Association's work. The other guiding principles, established to help change women's lives, are Equality of Opportunity, Participation of Young Women, Empowerment and Social Justice.

Multi-faith awareness

In the 'nineties, the diversity of faiths represented in the YWCA, particularly amongst the users of our services, became a key issue and challenged our policies of equal opportunities and non-discrimination. In the 21st century, we will need to encourage new ways of developing a greater understanding and respect for each other's faith traditions, as well as encouraging the spiritual perspective of our work.

✠ Endpiece

Reflections
Opportunities and Challenges

Endpiece

✠   'Earth's crammed with heaven,
        and every common bush aflame with fire,
        but only he who sees takes off his shoes,
        the rest sit round and eat blackberries'.

In these words Elizabeth Barrett Browning, in her poem *Aurora Leigh,* declares the belief that others can share Moses' experience of meeting God in transformative everyday experiences.

Such a feast gives glimpses of some of the ways in which twenty-first century Christians discover a heightened awareness of God. We read of three main strands. There is a range of personal devotion—of waiting on God in silence, in Bible study and prayer, of spiritual nourishment through music, art or poetry, and the use of symbols. There is the breadth and depth of public worship, with distinctive elements but often, surprisingly, common practices. Do those who are pursuing their spiritual journey alone realise what resources they could find in the churches—and do the churches realise what they have to offer?

Then there is an overwhelming acknowledgement of the influence of other people in spiritual nourishment—those who have been guides and encouragers on the Christian journey, and walked alongside offering comfort and also challenge. The description of Jesus as 'friend' (see John 15:12-15) is being rediscovered by feminist theologians, who suggest the model of 'Christian friendship' is helpful. The number of references to the importance of friends, of pastoral care, and of house groups and cell groups, in *Such a feast* may be a challenge to the churches to explore this further.

✠ For me, this text has brought into sharp focus just how much of Christian spirituality is common to every tradition represented here. Of course, prayer is the golden thread which binds us all together, but many other spiritual gifts are offered to the reader. I was moved by the intensely intimate and personal experiences described so frankly by individual Christians who have contributed to the second part of the book, and have been humbled by the degree of devotion revealed. The final section seems to me to exemplify how groups of like-minded Christians have come together to practise a spirituality of unity and to carry this out into the wider world.

It has been a privilege to be associated with this book.

✠ Eating isn't what it used to be. In my younger days we ate together as a family, the times set, the food predictable, familiar, traditional. All was orderly, routine, even ritual. It was a revelation to discover that others did not do the same, that our pattern was not standard, universal.

Awareness of the life and practices of other churches too came as a surprise, met with curiosity and a sense of being half-attracted, half-repelled. But contact with other Christians eventually created an appreciation of their traditions and, in due course, a willingness to explore some of them myself.

There has been a revolution in eating habits in my lifetime. What we eat, where we eat, when we eat, with whom we eat, is vastly different from an earlier pattern. And ecumenical developments have in a similar way opened up a world of varied experience, creating greater tolerance and fuller understanding.

Such a feast will help many Church people to know what is done and valued by others, and insights gained may not only create toleration but stimulate an appetite to taste for themselves. The real benefit of trying a new dish, however, cannot be obtained by a kind of 'take-away' eaten out of context, and Church practices without the appropriate ethos may seem odd and artificial.

The book tells us what is on offer and how it nourishes. My hope is that it will lead to more personal sharing in a setting of hospitality.

Too often ecumenical encounters produce a kind of hotpot which is not true to any one tradition. To share each other's specialities would be more adventurous and creative. For me, *Such a feast* is not to so much a description as an invitation.

✠ After the lengthy process of gathering in the material for *Such a feast,* suddenly we had the completed text to read. This put the contributions in a completely different context: they were no longer just interesting separate pieces but part of a whole picture of what it is that nourishes Christians up and down the land today.

And... wow! What a read! What a feast! The connections within the diversity, the richness and variety, all give me hope and encouragement as I seek to know and understand God in my everyday living and worshipping. This book has been an amazing project to be part of—full of surprises and blessings.

✠ This book identifies the Spirit's creative possibilities in both the interior and exterior life, both social concern and religious practice, both denominational commitment and freedom across boundaries of church and tradition. It demonstrates the value of Word and of Sign, the value of sharing and of withdrawing, the value of exuberance and of stillness, the value of struggle and of certainty. It celebrates being uplifted by both beauty in creation and the beauty of holiness.

Here we find the vertical divisions of the churches and the horizontal spread of new forms of worship. We find both searching and finding, both anger and peace. *Such a feast* shows how the 'Godness' of God is experienced in the lives of individuals, families, groups and communities. It is, at the same time, liberating, reassuring and demanding, and provides a feast of such diversity and richness that no-one need leave hungry.

✠ I have been involved with the material for *Such a feast* almost since I joined the Spirituality Co-ordinating Group over four years ago, because it all began with the members of that group sharing their own spiritual journeys as a way of getting to know one another.   It was immediately clear how much we had in common, whatever our denominational background;   and also that our diversity would prove to be our strength as a group.

Then if that was true for us—maybe a dozen people—might it not be true for those we represented?   Might they not also feel encouraged, challenged, inspired by such a calling together?   Out of this the book was born, though like many a birth, not smoothly.

How were we to pass to all our member organisations our own faith that this kind of sharing does not divide but strengthen?   How were we to draw in those members who felt that they sat on the edge of Churches Together in England?—yes, your voice matters just as much.   Would it be painful if individuals seemed to sit loosely to their own churches?   And what of those who drew nourishment from outside any church at all?   But yes, of course, there is the grit that creates the pearl, the discomfort that opens up more honest sharing by others.   And what of those who would rather **do** spirituality than talk about it?

Along this winding path we midwives have picked our way, gnashing our teeth and rejoicing by turns.   And now the baby has come fully into the world, and what a baby it is—what joy we feel, for it is an amazing child, set to challenge, encourage and inspire.

✠ Here is *Such a feast* of spiritual treasures. The title has been drawn from George Herbert's *The Call,* in which *the Feast* is Jesus Christ—*Come, my Way, my Truth, my Life. Such a Truth*, says Herbert, *as ends all strife.*

Such a feast celebrates the riches of diversity. Yet for many people spiritual nourishment is bound up with public worship, and forms of public worship have become deeply, personally ingrained, they have become inaccessible and inimical to strangers, they have been rallying points of conformity and bones of contention. Spirituality itself has been divisive rather than unitive.

So it is always important to look beyond the experience to the source of the experience. Experience is of God, not so much God-given as God who gives himself. It is Jesus Christ himself who is the Feast. Experience is that *Truth as ends all strife.* A book like this may make spiritual nourishment a topic to be researched, discussed and described, but ultimately for the Christian, God is not to be experienced but **is** the experience. It is God who is the active partner in experience, not the passive object.

This sense of the God who goes before us, the prevenient grace, is expressed beautifully in one individual voice:

> 'What can I do? I can do nothing he has not sanctioned and ordained. He is the air I breath, the beauty I see, and to give him less than all of me would be to cheat the one who is all to me.

> My spiritual journey, and its nourishment, is life. For God is my life. To lose God is to lose life. He is the author and finisher of my faith. He keeps me going; my life is priceless to him, and therefore to not acknowledge him means to not acknowledge life.'

Elsewhere, in his poem *Easter,* George Herbert celebrates the Resurrection (so powerfully set to music by Ralph Vaughan Williams in his *Five Mystical Songs*):

> *Rise, heart; thy Lord is risen.*
> *Sing his praise without delays.*

The initiative is always God's: his Son is *the Feast.*

Information and Addresses

Correspondence arising from **Such a feast** should be addressed to:
Judith Lampard, Churches Together in England, 27 Tavistock Square,
London WC1H 9HH. Tel: 020 7529 8141. www.churches-together.org.uk

Member Churches

Baptist Union of Great Britain
Baptist House
129 Broadway
Didcot
Oxon
OX11 8RT
Tel: 01235 517700
www.baptist.org.uk

Cherubim and Seraphim Council of
Churches
The Prayer House
175 Earlham Grove
Forest Gate
London
E7 9AP
Tel: 020 8534 5101

Church of England
Church House
Great Smith Street
London
SW1P 3NZ
Tel: 020 7898 1000
www.church-of-england.org

The Church of Scotland
121 George Street
Edinburgh
EH2 4YN
Tel: 0131 225 5722
www.churchofscotland.org.uk

Congregational Federation
4-8 Castle Gate
Nottingham
NG1 7AS
Tel: 0115-911 1460
www.congregational.org.uk

Council of African & Afro-Caribbean
Churches
31 Norton House
Sidney Road
London
SW9 0UG
Tel: 020 7274 5589

Council of Oriental Orthodox
Christian Churches
Church Square
34 Chertsey Road
Shepperton
TW17 9LF
Tel: 020 8368 8447

Ichthus Christian Fellowship
The Georgian House
31 East Dulwich Grove
London
SE22 8PH
Tel: 020 8299 5500
www.ichthus.org.uk

IMCGB
55 Tudor Walk
Watford
Hertfordshire
WD2 4NY
Tel: 01923 239266

Independent Methodist Churches
66 Kirkstone Drive
Loughborough
LE11 3RW
Tel: 01509 268566
www.imcgb.org.uk

Joint Council for Anglo-Caribbean
Churches
141 Railton Road
Brixton
London
SE24 0LT
Tel: 020 7737 6542

Lutheran Council of Great Britain
30 Thanet Street
London
WC1H 9QH
Tel: 0207 554 2900
www.lutheran.org.uk

Methodist Church
25 Marylebone Road
London
NW1 5JR
Tel: 020 7486 5502
www.methodist.org.uk

Moravian Church House
5-7 Muswell Hill
London
N10 3TJ
Tel: 020 8883 3409
www.moravian.org.uk

New Testament Assembly
5 Woodstock Avenue
Ealing
London
W13 9VQ
Tel: 020 8579 3841

Oecumenical Patriarchate
5 Craven Hill
London
W2 3EN
Tel: 020 7723 4787

Religious Society of Friends
Friends House
173 Euston Road
London
NW1 2BJ
Tel: 020 7663 1000
www.quaker.org.uk

Roman Catholic Church
38-40 Eccleston Square
London
SW1V 1BX
Tel: 020 7834 5612
www.tasc.ac.uk/cc

Russian Orthodox Church
Cathedral of the Dormition
   and All Saints
67 Ennismore Gardens
London
SW7 1NH
Tel: 020 7584 0096
www.sourozh.org

Salvation Army Territorial HQ
101 Newington Causeway
London
SE1 6BN
Tel: 020 7367 4500
www.salvationarmy.co.uk

United Reformed Church
86 Tavistock Place
London
WC1H 9RT
Tel: 020 7916 8645
www.urc.org.uk

Wesleyan Holiness Church
City Road
St Paul's
Bristol
BS2 8TX

Free Churches Group
Revd Geoffrey Roper, Churches Together in England, 27 Tavistock Square,
London WC1H 9HH. Tel: 020 7529 8141

Member Bodies in Association

Afro-West Indian United Council of
Churches
New Testament Church of God
Arcadian Gardens, High Road
Wood Green
London
N22 5AA
Tel: 020 8888 9427

Association of Interchurch Families
Inter-Church House
35-41 Lower Marsh
London
SE1 7SA
Tel: 020 7620 4444
www.aifw.org/aif.htm

Bible Society
Stonehill Green
Westlea
Swindon
Wiltshire
SN5 7DG
01793 418100
www.biblesociety.org.uk/

CHAD
50 Scrutton Street
London
EC2A 4XQ
020 7452 2085

Christians Aware
2 Saxby Street
Leicester
LE2 0ND
Tel: 0116 2540770
www.christiansaware.co.uk/

College of Preachers
10a North Street
Bourne
Lincolnshire
PE10 9AB
Tel: 01778 22929
www3.mistral.co.uk/collpreach

Focolare Movement
62 Kings Avenue
London
SW4 8BH
Tel: 020 8671 8355
www.focolare.org.uk

Iona Community
Pearce Institute
840 Govan Road
Glasgow
G51 3UU
Tel: 0141-445 4561
www.iona.org.uk/

L'Arche
10 Briggate
Silsden
Keighley
BD20 9JT
Tel: 01535 656186
www.larche.org.uk

Retreat Association
The Central Hall
256 Bermondsey Street
London
SE1 3UJ
Tel: 020 7357 7736
www.retreats.org.uk

Student Christian Movement
University of Birmingham Westhill
14-16 Weoley Park Road
Selly Oak
Birmingham
B29 6LL
Tel: 0121-471 2404
www.charis.co.uk/scm/index.htm

YMCA
640 Forest Road
London
E17 3DZ
020 8509 4577
www.ymca.org.uk

YWCA
Clarendon House
52 Cornmarket Street
Oxford
OX1 3EJ
Tel: 01865 726110
www.ywca.org.uk

Index

Affectionate welfare, *see* pastoral care
Agape, *see under* Lovefeast (s)
Alpha courses, *see under* training
Anointing, 29, 60, 64, 81
Architecture, 20, 64
Art, 20, 36, 56, 61, 107, 110, 127
   see also Icons
Awareness:
   of cultures, 138-9
   of difference, 138-9
   of disability, 136-7

Baptism, 11, 15, 19, 29, 31, 38, 50, 60, 64, 65, 73, 80, 115, 121, 131
   believers', 73, 75, 76
   infant (paedo-), 73
Bible:
   authority, 14, 17, 24-5, 27, 50, 63, 68, 78, 89, 91, 143-5
   ministry of the Word, 16, 18, 27, 31, 37, 39, 42, 43-4, 59, 67, 70, 73, 100, 104, 141, 142
   reading (private), 17, 20, 27, 86, 90, 96, 98, 100, 101, 122, 124, 125, 146
   study, 12, 15, 24-5, 27, 31, 32, 34, 39, 47, 70-1, 73, 76, 78, 85, 86, 96, 99, 100, 102, 110, 113, 114, 121, 122, 125, 134-5, 143, 159
Blessings, 63, 68
   Apostolic, 62
   Papal, 62
Broadcasting, 93, 126, 127
Buddhism, 108, 109, 112

Cell groups, *see under* meeting(s)
Celtic spirituality, 95, 125
Charismatic movement/renewal, 18, 62, 117
Chrismation, 29, 64
Christian Year, 18-19, 43-4, 52-3, 61, 63, 65, 123-4
Christingle service, 43

Community, Christian/church, 12-13, 27, 31-3, 35, 85, 89, 96, 97, 100, 101, 110, 113, 117, 126, 136-7, 157
   desire for, 152-3
   religious, 19, 64, 85, 110, 111, 134, 143-5, 146-8, 149-50, 153
   see also Iona, Taizé, worship, meeting for
Concern, *see* pastoral care, social concern
Confession, 38, 64, 121, 123
   see also repentance
Confirmation, 19, 50, 60, 121
Corrymeela Community, 153
Counselling, 15, 24, 33, 47
   see also pastoral care
Covenant:
   and Baptist Union, 11
   Covenant Service, 40, 41
Creeds, 14, 19, 63, 70

Dance, dancing, 23, 32, 47, 111
Devotional aids, *see* resources
Disability, *see under* social concern
Discipleship, 32, 72, 143, 144
Discipline, Christian, 11, 12, 16, 23, 27-8, 57, 64, 74
Drama, 32

Easter People, 13
Ecumenism:
   Baptist, 13
   Cherubim & Seraphim, 15
   Focolare, 143, 144
   individual, 85, 87, 144
   Iona Community, 146
   L'Arche, 149
   local, 103, 126
   Methodist, 40
   Moravian, 45
   Oecumenical Patriarchate, 30
   Salvationist, 69
   Student Christian Movement, 154
   United Reformed, 71

Education, *see* training
Eucharist, *see* Holy Communion
Evangelical Alliance, 31, 73
  Basis of faith, 31
Evangelism, 31, 32, 37, 41, 42, 45

Faith:
  growing in, 11, 87, 95, 96, 98, 119
  sharing, 24, 32, 93, 97, 108, 113,
    114, 117, 120, 121, 122, 123,
    125, 126
Fasting, 23, 27-8, 32, 39, 52, 63, 65,
  74, 87, 123
Fathers of the Church, 27, 29, 52, 65
Feasts, feasting, 63, 123
  see also Christian Year,
  Lovefeast(s)
Financial giving, tithing, 32, 74
  sharing, 146
Fox, George, 54, 56, 57, 112
Funeral rites, 19, 31

Healing:
  physical, 33
  services, 47, 73, 80-1, 126
  spiritual, emotional, 33, 87, 108,
    109, 112, 113, 150
Holy Communion (Eucharist), 15, 17,
  18, 19, 29, 31, 38, 39, 44, 47,
  50, 51, 58-9, 59-60, 61, 62, 63,
  75, 81, 100, 105, 115, 116, 117,
  119, 120, 121, 122, 127, 131,
  144, 149
Holy Spirit:
  fruits of, 31, 34, 35
  gifts of, 31, 35, 80, 125
  life in the, 35, 144
  manifested, 14, 16, 22, 23, 24, 25,
    34-5, 48, 58, 63, 64, 67, 87,
    123, 125
  see also spiritual gifts, spiritual
  nurture
Hymns, hymnody, 18, 21, 27, 32, 37,
  38, 40, 41, 43, 45, 51, 59, 70,
  77, 86, 121, 122

Icons, 28, 63, 64, 110, 123, 124

Ignatian spirituality, 56, 62, 85, 109,
  115
Incense, 20, 37, 64, 110, 124
Interfaith resources, *see under*
  resources
Iona Community, songs, 13, 70, 115,
  146-8, 153

Jewish spirituality, 125
Julian of Norwich, 107, 112

Keswick Convention, 13, 74, 102

Lay ministry, 19-20, 21, 33, 38, 104
Laying-on of hands, 80
  see also confirmation
Lectio Divina, 61
Liturgical Year, *see* Christian Year
Liturgy, 17-19, 26, 37, 43-4, 51, 58-9,
  59-60, 61, 63-4, 87, 115
  freedom in practice of, 13, 44
  of St James, 51
  see also Holy Communion
Lord's Supper, *see* Holy Communion
Love, ministry of, *see* pastoral care
Lovefeast(s), 40, 45, 67, 68
  Agape, 87

Marriage, 15, 19, 29, 31, 50, 60, 64,
  131-2
  development, 33
  preparation, 33
Mary, Our Lady, 53, 61, 144
Mass, *see* Holy Communion
Meditation, 39, 43, 45, 56, 61, 74,
  104, 105, 108-9, 122
Meeting(s):
  'Christian Conference', 39
  class, 39-40
  family, 48
  for fellowship, 39, 47, 99
  in band, 39
  in cell groups, 31, 41, 48, 76, 101,
    144
  in society, 39
  local church, 11, 71, 81, 126
  see also under worship

Membership, 11, 18, 29, 56, 76, 81
    see also baptism
Mentoring, *see* pastoral care, spiritual
    guidance
Metanoia, *see* repentance
Ministry, 15, 21, 24, 25, 33 34, 41,
    42, 141-2
    see also lay ministry, ordained
    ministry
Miracle(s), 16, 108, 118
Mission, 32, 40, 41, 45, 67, 68
Monasticism, *see under* community
Multi-faith resources, *see* resources:
    see also Buddhism
Music, 15, 20, 23, 27, 32, 37, 38, 43,
    47, 51, 56, 61, 63, 64, 86, 87,
    93, 94, 95, 101, 103, 105, 108,
    111, 115, 122, 124, 126, 127
    see also hymns, singing
Myers-Briggs Personality Type
    Indicator, 110, 141
Mysteries, *see* anointing, baptism,
    chrismation, Holy Communion,
    marriage, ordained ministry,
    repentance

Northumbria Community, 13, 134,
    153

Ordained ministry, 19, 21, 25, 29, 45,
    50, 60, 64, 73, 76
Orders (holy), 29, 45, 50, 60, 64
    see also ordained ministry

Pastoral care, 16, 24, 33, 47, 48, 49,
    71
Penance, 50, 60
Pilgrimages, 38, 53, 62, 64, 66, 122
Poetry, 32, 52, 94, 105, 107, 127
Prayer, 16, 17, 21, 23, 27-8, 31, 34,
    39, 43-4, 45, 47, 52, 53, 58, 59,
    60, 61, 62, 63, 64-5, 68, 69, 70,
    74, 76, 78, 80-1, 85, 87, 96, 97,
    98, 99, 100, 101, 104, 105, 106,
    107, 108, 110, 112, 113, 114,
    115, 117, 119, 120, 121, 122,
    123, 125, 126-7, 131, 134, 139,
    146, 158, 159
Jesus prayer, 28, 65
liturgical, 17, 27, 43-4, 45, 51, 53,
    58, 59, 61, 62, 63
personal, private, 12, 13, 19, 27-8,
    32, 34, 39, 47, 53, 60-1, 85, 95-
    6, 99, 100, 104, 115, 118, 120,
    126
traditions of, 56, 62, 70, 125
Preaching, 15, 37-8, 40, 47, 59, 73,
    78, 87, 96, 104, 120, 126, 141-2

Religious communities, *see under*
    community
Renewal, *see* revivals, spiritual
Repentance, 29, 35, 87
Resources:
    audio, video, film, 33, 86, 127, 134
    devotional, 20, 36, 38, 44-5, 54-5,
    56, 60, 62, 100
    interfaith, multi-faith, 85, 96, 112,
    160
    printed, 12, 17, 21, 32, 33, 41,
    44-5, 54-5, 64-5, 104, 112, 122,
    126, 157
    see also art, hymns, icons, liturgy
Retreats, 12, 61, 70, 85, 105, 109,
    112, 115, 119, 122, 151-3
Revivals, spiritual, 15, 23, 31, 38, 57

Sacramentals, 60
Sacraments, *see* anointing, baptism,
    confirmation, Holy Communion,
    marriage, orders (holy),
    penance, repentance, unction
Scriptures, *see* Bible
Silence, 54, 56-7, 61, 70, 85, 95, 105,
    106, 107, 108-9, 115
Singing, 23, 27, 37, 45, 47, 51, 70,
    87, 95, 101, 126, 147
    see also hymns, music
Social concern, 32, 39, 40, 42, 47,
    57, 59, 68, 71, 86, 100, 106,
    113, 138-9, 146, 154, 155,
    156-7, 159-60
    and disability, 136-7, 149-50, 154
Soul Survivor youth camp, 101

'Spiritual churches', 25
Spiritual gifts:
   exercise of, 11, 34, 48
   nurture of, 22, 34, 48
   see also under Holy Spirit
Spiritual guidance/direction, 24, 29,
   32, 48, 52, 61, 63, 64, 85, 108,
   151
   see also counselling, pastoral
   care, retreats
Spiritual nurture, 24, 25, 46, 50, 56,
   65, 85, 87, 100, 101, 105, 113,
   116, 119, 120, 125, 126, 132,
   135, 143-5, 146-8, 154, 155
Spring Harvest, 13, 74, 85
Suffering, 74, 144, 149
Syriac language, 51, 53

Taizé Community, chants, 62, 70, 95,
   115, 155
Testimonies, 24-5, 69, 73, 87, 111,
   113, 121
Tithing, *see* financial giving
Tongues, gift of, 125
Tradition, sacred/holy, 26, 27, 63,
   110
Training, 15, 21, 32, 33, 47, 74, 86,
   102, 114, 115, 116, 117, 118,
   119, 121, 126, 141-2
   Alpha courses, 32, 76

Unction, 50, 60
   see also anointing

Vestments, 20, 36, 37, 64
Via negativa, 107

Wesley, John and Charles, 39-40, 41
Word, ministry of the, *see under* Bible
Worship:
   as stimulus to spirituality, 93, 100,
     114, 146, 155
   meeting for, 11, 14-15, 18-19, 23,
     27, 31, 34, 36, 38, 41, 43-4,
     46-7, 56-7, 59-60, 63-4, 68, 70,
     73, 75, 78, 81, 95, 96, 99, 101,
     103, 104, 105, 107, 108-9, 110,
     112, 113, 115, 119, 122, 123,
     126
   style of, 17, 20, 23, 27-8, 32, 36,
     38, 43-4, 46-7, 54-5, 56-7, 58-9,
     63-4, 68, 70, 73, 78, 81, 87,
     105, 107, 110, 115, 123-4

Youth work, 15, 31, 48, 66, 79,
   154-5, 156-8, 159-60